I0151039

Lead Like a Woman

THE TOP TEN LEADERSHIP
MISTAKES WOMEN MAKE AND
HOW TO AVOID THEM

Dr. Angela D. Massey

Life On Purpose Publishing
An Angela Massey Imprint

WINDSOR, CONNECTICUT

Lead Like a Woman

THE TOP TEN LEADERSHIP MISTAKES WOMEN MAKE AND HOW TO AVOID THEM

Dr. Angela D. Massey

Gap Closer™ Publication

> A Division of Life On Purpose Publishing
> Windsor, Connecticut

Lead Like A Woman: The Top 10 Leadership Mistakes Women Make And How To Avoid Them/Dr. Angela D. Massey

ISBN 10: 0-9961908-5-6
ISBN 13: 978-0-9961908-5-5

Library of Congress Control Number: 2016912034

Dedications

First, this book is dedicated to my granddaughters: Jael and Sofia. May I leave you a legacy that empowers you to be everything you were meant to be!

Second, this book is dedicated all the women who paved the way and showed me what it means to lead like a woman: Mom, Grandma Catherine, Nana, my godmother: Mommy, Sister Thurma, Sister Bessie, Sister Blount, Aunt Chris, Aunt Carolyn, and Pastor Roz.

Third, this book is dedicated to the thousands of women who have attended my Women's Leadership Conferences and insisted that I "write a book about it!" . . . Thank you for pushing me in this direction; you have changed my life.

Finally, this book is dedicated to every woman who dares to see herself and be herself as she takes the reins of leadership.

Acknowledgements

Antoine, thanks for coaching me. You are an amazing leader and your input was invaluable. Adrian, thanks for all the help with this book. You are one gifted researcher and writer! Aaron, thanks for letting me "just read this to you" a million times. You never acted bored! You guys are the best sons a mom could ever have!

Cathy, I have watched you lead in your community, lead in your workplace, and lead in your family. Thank you for showing me what it means to be authentic and rolling up one's sleeves to get it done. You are my vault, my sounding board . . . my sister! DDD, Sug!

Faye and Lolitha, my sisters from another mother! Both of you continue to amaze me as I witness how gracefully you lead in your families and in your ministries. Thank you for being my sisters, my friends, and my prayer warriors. Who knew we would grow up to be doctors, pastors, and authors? God is good!

To my SiSTARS MasterMind:
- Star Bobatoon
- Gena Yuvette Davis
- Lisa Ann Landry
- Tarsha Polk
- Toni Harris Taylor
- Tish Times
- Nikki Woods

It is an honor to be associated with some of the most successful women in this industry. You ladies inspired me to get this done and I sincerely appreciate you!

My BFFs . . . you know who you are! I love you . . . yes, *you*! I cannot imagine where I would be without my special friends. Each of you gives so much in the name of friendship. I couldn't have written this book without you. You all are the bomb dot com!

My Sisterin' Prayer Group:
- Pastor Lydia "Pat"
- Pastor Jessie
- Sisterin' Ruby
- Sisterin' Carrie
- Sisterin' Rose
- Sisterin' Edith

Thank you for always praying me through. Your prayers continue to avail much!

Lisa Ann, I knew my intuition was on point when I asked you to write the foreword. See, I practice what I teach! You confirmed for me that both the message of this book and the method of delivery are timely, entertaining, and relevant. Thank you for writing the foreword even while you had out-of-town guests to entertain and a boatload of other things to do. You nailed it! Hail to Big Blue!

Attorney Candace Duff, I met you late in the process of finishing this project and we met under "other than worldly" circumstances. However, the timing was perfect! Thank you for the weekly accountability calls, for the feed-forward on the book cover, and for all of the information you shared with me on how to get the book out to the masses. You're a rock star!

Coach, I feel your positive energy! You made a huge positive impact on me, and I am eternally grateful. Thank you for being my silent cheerleader! Write your book.

Last, but not least, I want to thank God for my mother who passed away on October 18, 2015. "Mom, you always told me that I could do whatever I set my mind to. I know you're in heaven now, and I just believe you're proud to call me your daughter. I certainly hope so! I love you, Mom!"

Contents

Foreword

We are on the verge of another historical moment in this country's history with the current presidential race. This country for the first time ever may actually have a female president! She is not a perfect candidate. She is just as imperfect as any male presidential candidate. She has made mistakes, but she is highly qualified. Hillary Clinton has served as secretary of state, senator from New York, first lady of the United States, first lady of Arkansas, a practicing lawyer and law professor, activist, and volunteer. Her qualifications are undeniable. Her qualifications make her *the most qualified* Presidential candidate—dare I say—in history. I love how Cecile Richards, president of Planned Parenthood puts it, "It's literally that she brings decades of experience in foreign policy, in domestic policy, in advocacy, and she would start day one in the White House knowing exactly what needs to be done."

In the backdrop of all her stellar qualifications, Hillary Clinton has to deal with being considered the B word (you know the one I'm talking about) being bossy, being too manly, being questioned about her ambition and her appearance—all double-standards in the world of leadership. Why? Simply because she is a woman! If she were a man, these insignificant matters would not be a consideration. I look at her and wonder what female role models did she have to guide her? What resources did she have—like this book—to help her see the unique and special qualities that women leaders bring to the table? If her situation was anything like mine, she had great male mentors and role models pushing her to deny her female qualities of leadership and to lead more like a man.

With a master's degree in Management, just shy of the dissertation for a PhD in Management and nearly 14 years of experience at IBM—10 of those years in a leadership role, I have experienced similar challenges. Both at IBM and while working on my advanced degrees, most of the lessons I learned about leadership advocated male models of leadership. The IBM Service Division where I worked was a bastion of male dominance my entire career. I can't tell you how many times the men I worked with made me feel like I was crazy, inadequate, PMS-ing, this one actually made my temperature boil—an affirmative action hirer because I was a woman in leadership whose style of leadership was different than his.

When you read *Lead Like a Woman*, you will sigh in relief because it confirms that women lead differently than men, and it's **okay**! Not only is it okay, but Dr. Angela shares research that shows women's effectiveness as managers, leaders, and teammates outstrip the abilities of their male counterparts in 28 of 31 managerial skill areas. Thank you, Dr. Angela!

I've known of Dr. Angela for at least sixteen years and have had a close professional and personal relationship with her over the past three years. I am proud to be included in her exclusive circle because for as long as I have known of her, she is highly regarded in the community of professional speakers. She is no-nonsense, direct, and backs it up with research, education, and experience. For 20 years, just like Dr. A, I have traveled across the United States, Canada, Australia, and Japan to facilitate Women's Leadership Conferences. As I was reading *Lead Like a Woman*, I felt like Dr. Angela was right there in my Women's Leadership Conferences! It's obvious she heard the exact same issues that I heard from women leaders around the world. What an excellent job she has done capturing the common mistakes female leaders make and presenting them to you by writing *Lead Like a Women: The Top 10 Leadership Mistakes Women Make and How to Avoid Them.*

You will enjoy the quick read, her master story telling, and the science she shares confirming our uniqueness as leaders. No, this won't be like other leadership books you've read. I think you'll quite enjoy her sassy tips on how to keep doing it all wrong contrasted with her *Lead Like a Woman* tips to do it the right way. She slaps you with quotes that leave you stinging and thinking, for example, "A leader with integrity has one self, at home and at work, with family and with colleagues. Leaders without integrity are putting on an act." She will make you check yourself and ask yourself questions like "have I been showing up to work with sugar and spice one day and Evileen they next?" If the answer is yes, that lacks integrity. Not to worry, just continue reading for her tips on how to achieve integrity.

The *Lead Like a Woman* tips can be easily applied. One of my favorite tips is to get rid of the suggestion box and replace it with the suggestion flowchart. I foresee it discouraging stupid suggestions and encouraging creative thinking, problem-solving and increases in achieving corporate goals. I could tell you how it works, but you will just have to get your yellow highlighter ready and read *Lead Like a Woman: The Top 10 Leadership Mistakes Women Make and How to Avoid Them.* So go ahead and get started, you'll be glad you did!

Lisa Ann Landry
Avalon, Georgia
International Trainer
Social Media Strategist

Website: https://www/LisaAnnLandry.com
LinkedIn: https://www.linkedin.com/in/lisaalandry
Facebook: https://www.facebook.com/TheSNCCWay/
Google+: https://plus.google.com/u/0/+LisaAnnLandry
Twitter: https://twitter.com/LisaaLandry
YouTube: https://www.youtube.com/user/LisaaLandry
Author of *Content Marketing: How to Get Started*

Introduction

Many great books have been written on leadership, especially as the topic relates to women. I'm certain more will be written as we look back to observe the impact of some of the world's greatest women leaders such as business magnet, Oprah Winfrey; Pepsi-Co CEO Indra Nooyi; Facebook COO Sheryl Sandberg; Massachusetts Senator Elizabeth Warren; and former Secretary of State Hillary Clinton—just to name a few. Each woman is a great leader in her own right. Certainly, all of these women have earned the title of greatness because they have led work teams successfully in a male-dominated world. These women understand leadership dynamics and offer us valuable lessons we can learn from observing their leadership savvy.

So you may be wondering why another book on this topic? Well, as a corporate trainer, conference leader, motivational speaker, and business coach, I am amazed to hear of all the mistakes women make in the name of leadership. For example, a delightful woman in one of my *Effective Leadership Skills for Women* Conferences shared her ideas regarding the need for on-going training. Rhonda (not her real name) was a first-time and front-line manager for a fork-lift company. In this particular conference we were discussing the importance of developing team members through training. Rhonda looked at me and said, "Dr. Angela, these guys are fork-lift operators. All they need to know how to do is drive a fork-lift. It's a waste of time and money to send these guys to training!"

Unfortunately, I meet people like Rhonda all the time. So I thought *how about a tongue-in-cheek book on women and leadership?* You see, sometimes the absurdity of what we think or say is not so clear to us until we see it in writing!

Initially, that's what this book started out to be: a tongue-in-cheek book on women and leadership. However, it morphed into something more as I reflected on the leadership concepts I learned while working on my Organizational Leadership degree. I found myself seeking the answers to two burning questions:

- Do women have natural leadership skills? If so, what are they?
- Is there any science to prove conclusively that women are better leaders than their male counterparts?

Here are my answers:

- Yes, women do have *some* natural leadership skills and there is hard science and research to prove it.
- No, there is no conclusive science to prove that women are better leaders than men.

So my initial desire to highlight what women in leadership oftentimes do wrong and then show how to do it right based on science and research is what you're reading right now. It's been quite a journey—five years to be exact from this book's inception to the finished project.

In my *Effective Leadership Skills for Women* Conferences I teach participants that when presented with a challenge, find a solution. So as not to strictly focus on the negatives, I am taking my own advice in this book. Here's what you will find in *Leading Like a Woman: The Top 10 Leadership Mistakes Women Make and How to Avoid Them:*

First, I give a brief exposition of what I believe are the top ten mistakes women leaders make as they relate to leading a team. In my tongue-in-cheek manner, each mistake is written from two perspectives: the leader's perspective followed by the team member's perspective. I've taken the approach of telling you the mistake and then giving you the most relevant leadership tips amassed from my education, my years of facilitating leadership conferences, and my extensive research.

Second, you will find a *Lead Like a Woman* tip at the end of each chapter. Again, science proves that women have some natural leadership abilities, so I present the science and the research to help you recognize and synthesize the leadership qualities you possess as a woman.

Third, you will find a Leadership Self-Assessment page at the end of each chapter where you can jot down your thoughts. To get the most from this book, I suggest you identify your own proclivities (negative and positive), and record them. This list will come in handy once you download your *Lead Like A Woman Leadership Development Guide* designed to go along with the book. You can download your guide here: kbpbjz.bookhip.com. The link is also included again at the end of each chapter. Be sure to download your copy so you can evaluate your leadership skills. Take an honest look at your leadership skills; then, glean from your personal assessment and identify the things you need to do or stop doing to become the best leader you can be. The *Leadership Development Guide* will help you with this process.

Fourth, you will find *Lead Like a Woman: The Top 10 Mistakes Women Leaders Make and How to Avoid Them* an easy read. After facilitating at least a thousand conferences and seminars from as far as Japan to as close as Hartford, Connecticut—a mere five-minute drive from my home—I know that you don't have time to read a 300 page book. I want you to get what you need, implement it, and lead on!

Finally, by no means is *Lead Like a Woman: The Top 10 Mistakes Women Make and How to Avoid Them* intended to be an authority on such a complex subject as women in leadership. Nor is it meant to bash or degrade men in leadership. In fact, I believe that a good book on leadership should challenge its reader to change. It is my hope that this book will help you do just that.

Dr. Angela

Dr. Angela D. Massey "The Gap Closer"
Windsor, Connecticut

International Speaker
Corporate Trainer
Certified Professional Coach
Author:
- *Interview Skills: How to Get Hired NOW!*
- *Going the Distance: Success Strategies for Online Students*

Contact with me on social media:

Website: www.drangelamassey.com
Linkedin: https://www.linkedin.com/in/drangelamassey
FaceBook: https://www.facebook.com/drangelamassey
Twitter: https://www.twitter.com/drangelamassey
Google+: https://google.com/+AngelaMasseythegapcloser
YouTube:
https://youtube.com/c/AngelaMasseythegapcloser

Keep Them in the Dark

You may have seen a popular video that surfaced on *YouTube* a few years ago entitled, *What Did You Do to My Sign?* There are several versions online; here's the link to the one I'm referencing. Watch it later. https://www.youtube.com/watch?v=QYcXTlGLUgE.

In the meantime, allow me to paint the picture for you as I relate the details of the video.

An old blind man is sitting in front of the steps of an office building situated in what appears to be a busy downtown area. The man is a panhandler begging for money. He has a cardboard sign propped up next to him with the handwritten words, *"I'm Blind Please Help."* A tin can is placed near the sign to collect whatever those passing by decide to give him. He can hear footsteps and voices of the many people around him, but seldom does he hear the sound of coins dropping in the tin can or near his feet.

People pass by him throughout the day, and on occasion a kind stranger drops a coin near his tin can. For the most part, though, few give.

A young woman (I like to think she works in advertising) walks past and sees the blind man with his sign and tin cup. She also notices the many people passing by, completely unmoved, let alone stopping to give the old man any money. In fact, she wasn't moved to give him money either.

She walks back to the blind man, takes out a thick marker from her brief case, grabs his cardboard sign, flips it over and writes a new sign. Meanwhile, sensing that someone is nearby and hearing the scratching sound of the marker against the cardboard, the old man feels the young woman's shoes. My grandmother and my great-grandfather were blind, so I can relate to the man's gesture. You see, blind people rely on their other senses to help them identify their surroundings. I imagine the old man wants to know two things: Who is this stranger, and what is she doing to his sign?

The young woman places the new, improved version of her sign down next to old man's tin can and walks away. Immediately people begin dropping coins at the beggar's feet or near his tin can. Throughout the rest of the day, stranger after stranger gives the blind man money.

After a while, the young woman returns to see how much others have helped the blind man. Once again, he feels the shoes of the stranger and recognizes it is the same person that changed his sign earlier. He asked her, "What did you do to my sign?" Her reply, "I wrote the same, but different words."

What did the re-written sign say? It simply said, "It's a beautiful day and I can't see it."

Now, imagine that this particular panhandler was a part of a group of blind panhandlers who had been organized into a corporation to increase their profits. He has been going to this particular territory for the last few weeks with dismal results.

Frustrated by his lack of production, the blind panhandler begins to wonder:

- What is my role in the organization?
- What is my role on the team?
- Why was I not given adequate supplies? (He had questioned Suzette, his leader, about his inadequate supplies, i.e., a poorly written cardboard sign, a small tin cup. Suzette did not respond.)
- Why did Suzette withhold the resources I needed to get the job done? For example, why wasn't I allowed to get an approved sign from the advertising department?

Overall, he just had questions!

THE LEADER'S MISTAKE:
Withdraw and Withhold

When leaders like Suzette—the panhandler's boss—fail to tell the team what is expected, failure is imminent. If you want to kill your team before they ever get started, it's simple.

- Do not make any effort to explain to your team their role or function.
- Whenever they ask you, just say something like, "It's up to you to figure it out. That's why I put you on the team!"
- Make sure they remain in the dark when it comes to knowing why they are a part of the team or why the team was even created in the first place.

While you are at it, withhold the support and resources the team needs. Do not give them any human resources; do not give them any financial resources. Instead, give them unreasonable deadlines; let them know that they are not important. Ignore them. Give them little or no attention. Under no circumstances are you to show interest and whenever they come to you with a concern tell them to "get over it!"

THE TEAM MEMBER'S MISTAKE:
Put an "I" in Team

With the mantle of leadership comes the responsibility of leading. Recognizing and solving your own mistakes and shortcomings is only half the battle when it comes to being an outstanding leader. You also have to recognize the inner workings of your team.

Whether it is office politics, poor leadership examples from the past or plain sabotage—some team members do not play by team rules. Here are some warning signs of team members who are trying to keep other team members in the dark:

- They withhold information that could help the team. They never let anyone know what they know. When asked about what they know, they simply feign ignorance.
- They build negative cliques within the team, and share important information only with the members of their cliques.
- They always state their opinion and make it clear that not every team member is equal; therefore, they cannot be expected to assist other team members of lower stature.

HOW TO AVOID THIS MISTAKE:
"Why" is the Most Important Word

No one can dispute the rivalry that existed between then Senators Barack Obama and Hillary Clinton during the 2008 Democratic Party presidential primaries. Even after winning the popular vote (which does not guarantee the Presidency to the candidate who receives the most popular votes in all 50 states and the District of Columbia) and getting 17,493,836 primary votes, Clinton still lost to Obama. Yet, later she would serve in the Obama Administration as Secretary of State.

How did Clinton go from enemy to ally proving her worthiness to become a member of Obama's team? I believe what she did after losing the primary holds the answer and exemplifies the traits of a great leader who happens to be a woman.

Faced with the challenge of convincing her supporters (her team) to support Senator Obama's presidential bid, Clinton managed to do so by helping them focus on *why* they were on her team in the first place—to make sure the next president would be a Democrat. She also helped them understand that the task had not changed, only the face of the candidate. They were still responsible for ensuring a Democrat, Barack Obama, became president.

At the 2008 Democratic Convention in Denver, Clinton said this (in part) to her team:

"I'm here tonight as a proud mother, as a proud Democrat, as a proud senator from New York, a proud American, and a proud supporter of Barack Obama.

My friends, it is time to take back the country we love, and whether you voted for me or you voted for Barack, the time is now to unite as a single party with a single purpose. We are on the same team, and none of us can afford to sit on the sidelines. This is a fight for the future, and it is a fight we must win together . . . and you haven't worked so hard over the last 18 months or endured the last 8 years to suffer through more failed leadership . . . Barack Obama is my candidate and he must be our president . . .

I want you to ask yourselves: Were you in this campaign just for me? Or were you in it for the young Marine and others like him? Were you in it for that mom struggling with cancer while raising her kids? Were you in it for that boy and his mom surviving on the minimum wage? Were you in it for all the people in this country who feel invisible? . . . Now, this will not be easy, progress never is, but it will be impossible if we don't fight to put a Democrat back into the White House."

As a leader, particularly as a woman, it is imperative that you clearly state your expectations, and the expectations of your organization from the very beginning. The team has a right to know so that they can respond in kind.

Hillary Clinton let her team of supporters know that she expected them to follow her lead and support the Democratic nominee. When Barack Obama became her candidate, she set the expectation that Barack Obama must become her supporters' candidate as well. She also let her team of supporters know that the organization—the Democratic Party—needed their support to ensure Obama's eventual victory.

Let's take this out of the political arena and bring it into the average workplace with a simple example: If you want your team to find a way to reduce costs by 10%, tell them and tell them why. It is always easier to navigate, especially when you know where you're going and why you're making the trip!

Additionally, providing feedback and recommendations allow team members to make the adjustments needed to keep the team on course.

Remember the story of the blind panhandler and this phrase: "Illumination is clarification!" Keeping your team in the dark creates unproductiveness, and an unproductive team is a direct reflection upon you, their leader.

LEAD LIKE A WOMAN
Support Connections

The characteristics of a destructive team member can be erosive. Left to their own destructive devices, these types of team members will continually divide the team. What can you do?

It is essential to your leadership campaign that you identify and correct destructive behavior immediately. In an effective organization you cannot have the blind leading the blind. So, what can you do to keep the blinders off?

Be vigilant in determining and controlling the make-up of team cliques. It is important that your team have connections with one another. Under the right circumstances team cliques should be accepted and allowed. Now, go back and read that again. I'm talking about positive cliques *not* negative ones!

A clique, according to Merriam-Webster is "a small group of people who spend time together and who are not friendly to other people." I want you to ignore the latter part of that definition and hear me out.

Experts tell us that women possess the natural ability to network and support. In fact, Helen Fisher, a contributor to the book entitled *Enlightened Power* says that, "women form cliques and regard power as an egalitarian network of supportive connections." Women, unlike men, tend to see themselves as equal to others—not above or below. Further, in a general sense, women have no problem supporting others.

Positive cliques can contribute greatly to the team in several ways, namely:

- They can pull the team together.
- They can help the team develop a stronger bond.
- They can build a sense of solidarity.
- They can increase the team's overall confidence.
- They can increase the team's overall productivity.

Julie Tappero sums up this point nicely, "If the clique is a complete team with a job to accomplish, it can boost creativity and help the team achieve higher goals."

The flip side, of course, to a positive clique is a negative clique. You and I both know that a negative clique can only poison the team. They counteract the much needed element of trust on the team; negative cliques reinforce doubt and increase levels of disrespect among the team members towards one another and towards the leader. Negative cliques backstab, gossip, and drain the team's energy. Additionally, negative cliques also bring to fore the negative "office politics" we all try so desperately to avoid.

Lead like a woman and use your natural ability to network and support, especially if you want your team to coalesce. Encourage positive cliques that provide supportive connections for your team and make sure you discourage the negative ones!

LEADERSHIP SELF-ASSESSMENT

How do you measure up? Use this page to objectively assess yourself and your team. Download your Leadership Assessment Guide at: kbpbjz.bookhip.com

Confusion Rules the Day

The story goes that one Saturday, on a football field in Anywhere America, a high school football game was played. There were two teams: the Marauders and the Tigers. On this Saturday it was obvious to any observer who the better team was.

The Tigers dominated the Marauders, and it was clear that it wasn't from being more talented. The Marauders seemed bewildered on the field. There was no continuity in their play. Plays that were meant to go left went right, and plays that were meant to go right went left. Players were out of position. In the huddle everyone tried to call out a play. Overall, the Marauders seemed befuddled and mystified on the field.

What made this game significant? Both teams were battling to make it to the championship. What made this game intriguing? For unknown reasons one team seemed to play completely out of sorts.

The Marauders had been without a coach for three weeks prior to the game. Their last coach had quit, and it took the school a week to hire a new one. The new coach had no experience, and she was in over her head. She didn't understand what it took to guide her players to victory.

For the two weeks prior to the championship game the players did nothing. No practices, no team motto, no problem. Whenever the players on the team showed any concern for Coach and her techniques, she told them "don't worry about it; you wouldn't understand. It's over your head." Was it a surprise that the Marauders were embarrassed?

THE LEADER'S MISTAKE:
Allow Confusion to Prevail

Bad things happen when confusion rules the day. A confused team is a team doomed to failure. To ensure your failure as the leader, simply make sure they do not understand the strategy of the team or even that the team *has* a strategy. Make sure they are ignorant of the organization's goals, principles, and values. If they are ignorant, they are not responsible, and neither are you. You can do this several ways:

- Never create a goal and mission statement for your organization.
- Keep the goal and mission statement a secret *only* shared with those at the top.
- Discourage team members from showing concern for what big brass is doing. After all, it has nothing to do with the price of tea in China or with your team's understanding where it fits into accomplishing corporate goals.

THE TEAM MEMBER'S MISTAKE:
Become the Authors of Confusion

When the torch of leadership is passed on to you, organization and order are qualities expected of women leaders. In fact, society tends to associate certain qualities with female leaders and still a different set of qualities with male leaders. For example, male leaders are expected to be competitive, domineering and aggressive, while female leaders are expected to be consensus-driven, compassionate, helpful, and nurturing.

If women do, in fact, have an innate B.S. barometer, the time to use it is when you're dealing with team members who purposely confound and confuse. Recognizing and dealing with these team members could mean the difference in how smoothly your team runs, to how fast you are run out of the office. There are signs to recognizing the team members I affectionately call *Confounding Confucius*. These confusing team members are easily spotted:

- They create confusion by allowing their emotions to rage out of control (especially in team meetings).
- When asked questions about projects, they point fingers at other members and give excuses as to why their project is in the pitiful state it's in. For example:

Leader: "What's the status of the project, and when is it going to be done?"

Confounding Confucius: "Oh, the status of the project . . . why don't you ask Susie? She's the one holding the project up."

- They seem to have no rules of civility, they refuse to talk during meetings, being reticent and offering a lot of one-liners.
- They have been known to leave right in the middle of something important.

HOW TO AVOID THIS MISTAKE:
Publicize the Team's Goal(s)

Again, I'd like to focus on something then Secretary of State Hillary Clinton said during her first speech to State Department employees to help you see the importance of articulating your team's goal.

> *"There are three legs to the stool of American foreign policy: defense, diplomacy, and development. And we are responsible for two of the three legs. And we will make clear, as we go forward, that diplomacy and development are essential tools in achieving the long-term objectives of the United States. And I will do all that I can, working with you, to make it abundantly clear that robust diplomacy and effective development are the best long-term tools for securing America's future."* Secretary of State Hillary Clinton

In my travels as a conference and keynote speaker I've met too many women who tell me their goals are in their heads. Pardon me, but *if it's in your head, you're still in bed! You're asleep!* Women leaders have to clearly articulate to their team the goal(s) and mission statement. If you have not taken the time to formulate your goals and mission statement, get your team together right now and work on getting this done.

Here's why you need to do this now: If you have a vision for your team, (and I certainly hope you do) that vision is meaningless if your team does not know that the vision exists. It's been said, "Where there is no vision, the people perish." Further, if you're heading a team ignorant of or out of touch with the goals, your team and your company will die a slow and painful death.

Like Hillary Clinton, you must remember that effective women in charge understand that the only reason a team exists is to accomplish a specific and common goal; therefore, they will utilize members to set and commit to the team's goals.

Never forget the story of the coach: A lesson in confusion can cost a championship run. It can ruin it. Whether you are building confusion purposely or accidentally it can be a career killer. It shows a lack of organization and leadership skills. Confusion is a career killer—yours and your team members!

LEAD LIKE A WOMAN
Trust Your Intuition

It is an undisputed fact that confusion is the basis for chaos; furthermore, it is the antithesis of organization. Team members that tend to react this way by creating confusing situations have to be removed or rehabilitated.

Being an effective woman in charge means you must tune up and turn up your confusion radar. What is your confusion radar? Simply put, it is your natural ability to rely on your intuition. Dr. Helen Fisher says that women "tend to think in webs of factors, not straight lines." She calls this feminine way of reasoning, *web thinking* which "enables them [women] to exercise more intuition—and intuition plays a productive, if often unrecognized, role in managerial decision making." According to Fisher, women's web thinking helps them to use their intuitive brain more than men. Now I don't know if women use their intuition more than men, but I do know that there is a great deal of science to support the fact that women should trust their gut as it relates to business.

Here's the scientific research:

> "Scientists have discovered that humans appear to have two, very different 'operating systems.' System 1 is our quick, instinctual, and often subconscious way of operating—it is controlled by our right brain and by other parts of our brain that have been around since prehistoric times, known as the "limbic" and reptilian" parts of our brain. System 2 is our slower, more analytical, and conscious way of operating—it is controlled by our left brain and by newer parts of our brain that have only developed since prehistoric times (also known as the "neocortex"). Researchers have found that intuition is part of System 1, which is why it comes on so rapidly and often does not make rational sense to us. In other words, intuitive decisions are not something that we have thought out carefully with reason, but rather choices that have arisen quickly out of instinct.

> But why, exactly, should we trust our gut instinct? One reason would be because researchers have found that System 1 often knows the right answer long before System 2 does."

Once you've observed Mr. or Ms. Confounding Confucius and you feel intuitively that he or she can poison the team, don't be afraid to address the behavior. Remember, intuition is part of your make up as a woman; you have it for a reason—trust it and use it!

Make sure that Confounding Confucius understands your goals. Their correct interpretations are vital to keeping them in sync with fellow team members. Reinforce Confounding Confucius's ability to speak his or her mind. Voicing their thoughts may create conflict, but often it can result in a more harmonious and authentic team experience.

Keep this in mind: questions lead to answers. Always validate your team's right to ask questions. Ignorance is not bliss, and can be used as a means of confusion which is what you don't want!

Lead like a woman and tap into your intuition and trust your gut, because doing so leads to better outcomes than trusting your logical, thinking brain alone!

LEADERSHIP SELF-ASSESSMENT

How do you measure up? Use this page to objectively assess yourself and your team. Download your Leadership Assessment Guide at: kbpbiz.bookhip.com

It's Not My Job!

The story goes that sometime, close to a battlefield over 200 years ago, a man in civilian clothes rode past a small group of exhausted battle-weary soldiers digging an obviously important defensive position. The section leader, making no effort to help, was shouting orders, and threatening punishment if the work was not completed within the hour.

"Why are you are not helping?" asked the stranger on horseback.

"I am in charge. The men do as I tell them," said the section leader, adding, "Help them yourself if you feel strongly about it."

To the section leader's surprise the stranger dismounted and helped the men until the job was finished. Before leaving the stranger congratulated the men for their work, and approached the puzzled section leader.

"I would tell you to notify top command next time your rank prevents you from supporting your men, but there is no need for that because you are being demoted to the rank of those very same men," said the stranger.

The year was 1780, and America was embroiled in a war for freedom with England. To be able to have any chance to win the war the colonies needed full investment from the soldiers as well as the command.

The stranger that appeared on horseback to help the battle-weary group of soldiers was none other than General George Washington. Of course, digging foxholes was not the General's job, but it was. It was obvious to General Washington that the section leader did not understand the mission, or the value of teamwork to achieve goals. The example of the section leader proved to be a turning point of the war.

THE LEADER'S MISTAKE:
Undervalue Team Members

If the team members don't want to be on the team, no problem! Make sure that they know the team's mission is not that important; therefore, they do not have to be committed to accomplishing the mission nor do they have to care about the outcomes. As long as your team members understand that what they do for the organization will go unvalued, you will never have to worry about them making a commitment. Should team members confuse this issue of recognition, expecting you to acknowledge their contributions, all you have to do is:

- Refuse to spend any time helping them to develop their skills.
- Douse their excitement, i.e., whenever they make a suggestion just look at them with the "that's really stupid" look on your face. They will get the message.
- Do not challenge them. In other words, let them continue to do the same thing, the same way, at the same time.
- Give them boring, mundane, thoughtless tasks; that way, your team members will never commit to your team.

THE TEAM MEMBER'S MISTAKE:
Who's Afraid of Commitment?

You are a distinguished leader, a woman who is devoted to advancing her career. It is vital to the operation of your team that members exhibit acceptable levels of commitment. Being able to understand team members' attachment and involvement is tantamount to your success. If you have fostered an environment that is conducive to commitment recognizing these team members should be easy.

If you have not then it could be a little more difficult. Here are a few signs:

- They do not take on any responsibilities, especially extra ones.
- If ever asked to pitch in with another team member, they make it clear it's not their job.
- They show up late for meetings.
- They leave early, and rarely finish assignments in time for meetings.
- When their behavior is questioned, they always reply they're swamped with work or use some other excuse to get you to leave them alone.

HOW TO AVOID THIS MISTAKE:
Roll up Your Sleeves and Have your Team's Back!

When it comes to getting the job done it takes a complete effort from the whole team. Yes, you are the leader; however, you are still a part of a team. Recognizing and understanding your role helps your team claim ownership. Think of your team as a mirror. When you look into the mirror you should see your reflection. The team's mission, your level of commitment, and value to the organization should be what you see. The greatest generals know that they've only achieved greatness because of great soldiers.

Speaking of soldiers, I am a proud American Veteran. I served in the U.S. Army. So imagine my delight when First

Lady Michelle Obama joined more than two hundred ac-
tive-duty, retired-military, veteran, and reservist women at
the Women Veterans Career Development Forum held on
November 10, 2014. The career forum focused on transi-
tioning to civilian life. I did not attend the Forum; however,
I made it my business, as a female veteran, to know what
happened and how it affected female veterans.

I mention this in this chapter because of something First
Lady Obama said:

> "But most of all, I want to thank all of you, the service mem-
> bers and veterans who have stood up every time this country
> has called. And before I go any further, I want to say two
> words that I don't think we can say enough, and that is,
> thank you. Thank you, thank you, thank you. Thank you
> for your service. Thank you for your sacrifice. Thank you
> for your unending commitment to our country.
>
> But I'm here today because I know that simply saying thank
> you isn't always enough. We're here because of wom-
> en...with distinguished records of service who still struggle
> to find jobs after they leave the military . . . .
>
> You might have your ups and downs. but I want you to
> know that this whole country believes in you, and **we've got
> your backs**. So we're going to keep rallying this country to
> serve you as well as you've served us."

You may or may not see the First Lady as a great female
leader—that doesn't really matter. I want you to see her
willingness to admit that it was her job and the job of others

to remedy the problem of female veterans who "still struggle to find jobs after they leave the military."

To support veterans in their transition to meaningful employment, during the Forum the First Lady announced two significant public-private partnerships with LinkedIn and Coursera that would help military members find and land the jobs they want. She showed me, a female veteran, not only *that* she had my back, but *how* she had my back.

Remember, the leader who rolls up her sleeves and gets in the trenches is the leader that inspires commitment from her team. I could think of no better example than that of yes, you guessed it—Former Secretary of State Hillary Clinton who went undercover in 1972. Here's the story as told by Amy Chozick in *The New York Times* about Hillary Rodham, Covert Operative:

> *"Playing down her flat Chicago accent, she told the school's guidance counselor that her husband had just taken a job in Dothan, that they were a churchgoing family and that they were looking for a school for their son. The future Mrs. Clinton, then a 24-year-old law student, was working for Marian Wright Edelman, the civil rights activist and prominent advocate for children. Mrs. Edelman had sent her to Alabama to help prove that the Nixon administration was not enforcing the legal ban on granting tax-exempt status to so-called segregation academies, the estimated 200 private academies that sprang up in the South to cater to white families after a 1969 Supreme Court decision forced public schools to integrate. Her mission was simple: Establish*

whether the Dothan school was discriminating based on race.

Make no mistake. Even in 1972, this took considerable guts. The segregated academies were the outward sign of the vicious backlash against the triumphs of the Civil Rights Movement that only would intensify over the following decade as the Republican party, and the conservative movement that would come to be its essential life-force, discovered that, in many important ways, the whole country was Southern. The backlash was even more virulent at the local level. If Undercover Hillz blew her cover, very bad things could have happened to her.

"It was dangerous, being outsiders in these rural areas, talking about segregation academies," said Cynthia G. Brown, a longtime education advocate who did work similar to Mrs. Clinton's."

I think this story illustrates beautifully the concept of having your team's back. Granted, Mrs. Clinton did not have a team in 1972; however, she sought to understand the problem from ground zero. This and other experiences would later help Clinton achieve a remarkable commitment from voters—especially the African-American female voter in her 2016 bid for president. Huffington Post reported, "Clinton's support among black women voters is even more significant since they have turned out at the highest rates of any race/gender subgroup in the past two presidential elections." While I have no firm data to explain why black women voters made a commitment to Clinton, I can only surmise that it has been, in part, because of her willingness to show women of color that she understands their plight and she's willing to roll up her sleeves to make things better.

You cannot force people to commit. Commitment develops when people feel involved and valued. Create a safe environment that allows team members to contribute without fear of ridicule. Remain sensitive to creating opportunities for participation and witness how members take ownership for the outcome. Lastly, help your team get the job done; after all, you are their mirror!

LEAD LIKE A WOMAN
Be a Holistic Leader

Of course each team member has a job description that clearly spells out what's expected of them. However, you have to make this phrase "other duties assigned" a part of your motto. What if it read like Southwest Airlines job descriptions: ". . . and whatever you need to do to enhance the overall operation." Okay. You can't change the job description but you can operate as if this were a phrase of empowerment and not of imprisonment.

Science confirms that women think differently than men, but you already knew that; didn't you? Fisher says that, "Women tend to generalize, to synthesize, to take a broader, more holistic, more contextual perspective of any issue." Your goal, as a leader, is to inspire commitment from your team. You inspire commitment when you lead from a holistic point of reference.

Sonia McDonald, author of *Holistic Leadership Understanding the Approach,* defines holistic leadership as "the ability for a leader not only to understand oneself and lead others from this vantage point, but also the premise that each of us must strive throughout our lifetime to become a centered individual who is able to effectively use the principal components of leadership."

Take a look at McDonald's *Seven Fundamental Assumptions of Holistic Leadership,* check one or two off, and work towards being, doing, or having that.

> *Holistic leadership proffers seven fundamental assumptions about the nature of effective leadership:*
>
> 1. *Successful outcomes result from an orientation toward development.*
>
> 2. *The healthiest and most productive development is done collaboratively.*
>
> 3. *The leadership unit shapes the context of collaboration.*
>
> 4. *The core leadership unit is the individual, which makes every participant a leader within his or her own sphere of influence.*
>
> 5. *The intrinsic desire for meaningful purpose suggests that every individual wants to realize his or her best potential.*

6. *Holistically-led collaboration requires that the participant's right to self-determination be respected.*

7. *The exercise of self-determination in a way that realizes the individual's best potential, results from an iterative process that must be supported.*

By reinforcing empowerment, you allow full career investment from team members. Think of these actions as your permission to your team to be self-directed, and go above and beyond the call of duty. Here's how:

Encourage team members to speak up and share ideas. Support volunteering amongst team members for projects that are unassigned.

Promote collaboration among team members, with the ultimate goal being working with other team members to successfully complete projects.

During my time at IBM I was fortunate enough to work for a young woman named Lynn. What I remember most about her leadership style was her ability to create a strong sense of belonging. She was self-assured and in turn created a self-assured team. It was nothing for her to roll up her sleeves, sit down at a computer, and help us process orders if we were up against a tight deadline. However, we always knew that she was our leader—not just another co-worker. Although she never said it, I believe she believed in the Three Musketeers motto: "All for one and one for all." We were committed to her, the team, and the organization. By the same token, we knew that Lynn was committed to us.

She was adept at seeing all of the parts while still seeing the whole. Lynn modeled a holistic leadership style and that style yielded great results.

Lead like a woman and use your natural ability to approach matters in a more holistic manner. As a woman you are naturally inclined to generalize, to synthesize, and to take a broader, more holistic, more contextual perspective of any issue. This naturally ability lends itself to holistic leadership which is a powerful way to gain commitment from your team. Go for it!

LEADERSHIP SELF-ASSESSMENT

How do you measure up? Use this page to objectively assess yourself and your team. Download your Leadership Assessment Guide at: rbpbjz.bookhip.com

Everyone is Inadequate

In a land far away in a faraway time there was a princess. She was renowned throughout the kingdom for her fashion sense. Every year the knights of the moon sponsored a fashion festival. It was known throughout the kingdom that the princess would do anything to win the best dressed award.

She put her team of advisors and yes women on alert that she was pulling out all the stops. With six months to plan, the dress would be perfect.

At first the process was relatively easy, the princess would tell her team what she wanted and they would do it. When she needed fabric she would tell her yes women who to get it from. When she needed the dress to be designed she let her advisors do it.

To the kingdom it seemed that the princess splendid dress would be made. We all know everything isn't always what it seems. As the months got shorter the princess got more involved, to be honest she took over.

The princess demanded to go to the beach and search for the pearls she needed. She sailed to Italy to get the fabric required. She took sewing classes so she could sew the dress. By the time she finished the classes, sailing around the world, and getting the tailor, the festival had passed. Because of her obsession with having the perfect dress, and her unwillingness to trust her assistants she missed the festival, and her dream was unrealized.

THE LEADER'S MISTAKE:
Be a Control Freak

If you want to ensure a heavy workload for yourself and a feeling of inadequacy in your team members do this: As a team leader, instead of delegating, simply do it all yourself. After all, if you want it done right you have to do it yourself, right? Take the position of know-it-all, since as a know-it-all you can maintain complete control.

Another way to make your team members feel inadequate is to select the wrong people to be on your team. To accomplish this make sure that you put your friends on the team even though your friends are not qualified. You can even practice nepotism here! Once you move outside of your family and friends, choose the know-it-all type because they can be very destructive to a team.

The know-it-all will work very hard to make other team members feel inadequate. When team members meet to exchange ideas and strategies, the know-it-all tends to be very condescending. There is no better way to help other team members feel inadequate than putting them on the team with someone who will make them feel small and insignificant. Know-it-alls are self-assured, self-directed, and self-sustaining (all great qualities, by the way) because they believe they don't need others; consequently, they will do an extraordinary job of alienating the other members.

THE TEAM MEMBER'S MISTAKE:
I Know Everything

Who likes a know-it-all? The answer is no one likes a know-it-all because he or she is a detriment to the team. Telltale signs you have a know-it-all on your team:

- She is a control freak.
- He talks down to other team members
- She starts every other sentence with, "As a matter of fact . . . "
- He will do another team member's job and justify his behavior by implying he did it because the team member could not be trusted to do it right.
- She talks more than she listens.

- He tends to be close-minded and unwilling to discuss other team member's ideas.
- She is opinionated to the extreme and doesn't mind sharing her strong opinions whenever the opportunity presents itself.

HOW TO AVOID IT:
Eight D's to Effective Delegation

In my *Women's Leadership Conferences* the topic of delegation is one that most are eager to learn how to do, but anxious when it comes to actually doing it. Before I give you the process of delegation, I want you to promise me that you will learn and use this affirmation when fear overtakes you and you just want to do the task yourself: "If I want it done right, I need to delegate it!" Don't be like the princess and miss a deadline because you are unwilling to trust your team to get the job done.

Now, here are the eight D's to effective delegation I teach in my conferences:

1. **Document**. Sit down and define the task in detail. Employ the first habit of a highly effective person and *begin with the end in mind*.

2. **Decide**. Take a good look at your team and each person's capabilities, and then choose the right person to handle the task. This is a critical step because if you decide on the wrong person you are setting

that person up for failure, as well as setting the team up for failure.

3. *Describe*. Make sure your team member has a clear, accurate, and detailed description of the assignment. I suggest that you write it down to avoid misunderstandings later.

4. *Demystify*. It baffles my mind when someone tells me they were given a task and little or no authority to get it done in a timely manner. You should explain your team member's level of authority; for example, can she make decisions without consulting you? What are her boundaries? Do you expect her to do a certain part of the job and then get back to you with the results? Can she get help from other team members with the project?

5. *Depend*. You have to trust your team member to get the job done. Depend on his level of commitment to you, your organization, your team, and the task at hand. Make sure that you express your confidence in his ability to get the job done.

6. *Direct*. While working on the task, your team member should feel comfortable coming to you to ask for your input. Make sure that you establish appropriate check points while the task is being completed. Let him know that he has a direct line to you and any assistance you can provide.

7. *Develop*. Assign tasks that have the potential to develop the skills of your team members. There's

nothing worse than being tasked with a grunt assignment.

8. ***Distinguish***. This final step occurs once the task has been completed successfully. Recognize and reward your team member for doing a great job, especially if the assigned task was sizeable and complicated. Show your appreciation.

LEAD LIKE A WOMAN
Be a Long-term Planner

Research suggest that women are naturally wired to "access multiple, complex scenarios and plot a long-term course." The ability to engage in long-term planning is critical to delegating tasks in a fair and equitable manner to ensure the job gets done.

Effective delegation is nothing more than long-term planning. In part, Businessdictionary.com defines long-term planning as an "exercise aimed at formulating a long-term plan, to meet future needs…" Each time you determine the need to delegate a task, you are engaging in long-term planning because you are formulating a plan to meet the needs of your organization.

Women who are striving to distinguish themselves in business understand the complexities of being a leader. Striving for perfection in leadership is perfectly normal, but you have to be aware of the trappings of your own ego. Effective leaders never try to do everything. Scholars tell us that effective leaders are good delegators, because they realize that sometimes completing a project takes more than one set of hands.

One area of caution: when you delegate a task, allow your team member to get the task done in a way that is most productive for her. Even if it takes her longer than it would have taken you, put your focus on the fact that the job was done and not on *how* the job was done. For example, if it takes Sarah two hours to do something that you could do in an hour, you have to allow Sarah the two hours as long as she gets it done. Then you can use it as a learning experience and show her how to get it done in an hour the next time the task is assigned to her.

When you approach delegation from results versus process, your team members develop a valuable skill, develop a sense of pride, and develop a deeper loyalty to you, to the team, and to the organization.

One more thing: Sometimes the by-product of delegation is the creation of a know-it-all. It is prudent when delegating to make sure that you specify the tasks you want completed. You should only delegate duties to which you have invested the time to explain with granular detail. Your team members should be taught the importance of never learning enough.

Lead like a woman and use your predisposition to plan long term to help you delegate the right task to the right person. Remember, as I stated earlier, effective delegation is nothing more than long-term planning and science says you're wired for that!

LEADERSHIP SELF-ASSESSMENT

How do you measure up? Use this page to objectively assess yourself and your team. Download your Leadership Assessment Guide at: kbpbjz.bookhip.com

Forget About Accountability

Coach Al Johnson related the following: "You call this fresh fruit?" I scolded the waitress who delivered a bowl of faded honeydew and overripe cantaloupe that the kitchen had, and for some reason, thought I would eat. I expected her to tell me it wasn't her fault.

"No," she agreed, "it doesn't look fresh to me, but the kitchen is almost out of fresh fruit. My apologies." It's not often that I'm at a loss for words, but at that moment, I couldn't speak. I knew she wasn't the chef, and it wasn't her fault, yet she apologized.

As I searched for words, the waitress directed my attention to the plump, red strawberries that garnished the sandwich platters my friends had ordered. "How about a big bowl of those?" she offered. I licked my lips in anticipation.

She returned in a hurry, eager to salvage my meal. But steps away from our table, she stumbled over a kink in the carpet and released the bowl, sending strawberries flying all over my dinner companions and me. They landed in our hair, on our shoulders, on our laps, and even in our purses. I was at a loss for words for the second time that night.

"Strawberries for everyone, I'll get the whip cream!" Lindsey declared, as she started to laugh. Her laughter was contagious and it infected my dining party.

This unflappable waitress helped us pick strawberries out of our hair and sped back to the kitchen to slice up some more. This time, I got to eat them instead of using them to make my hair look pretty.

We left her a huge tip, this young waitress who spilled food all over us.

As we left, I pulled her aside. "You didn't get upset when I scolded you for the not so fresh cantaloupe and honeydew. You didn't get frustrated or upset when you tripped and made sure everyone enjoyed the strawberries. You didn't blame the kitchen, or the carpet. You just handled it. How did you do that?"

"Well," she answered. My boss says if the customer is not satisfied it is a direct reflection upon me. I'm responsible for making sure you come back," she explained. "You'll base your decisions on my actions."

She was responsible for every mess she made. She was responsible for serving me the faded honeydew and over-ripe cantaloupe. She was responsible for tossing strawberries all over my friends and me.

Moral: This waitress learned the lesson of accountability from her boss. That profound example taught her that taking total responsibility for herself, her job, her relationships, and her behavior is the key to performing her job. Is it any wonder that people stand in line to wait to be seated in Lindsey's section?

THE LEADER'S MISTAKE
I Can't Be Held Responsible

In 2013, Dr. Linda Sapadin coined the phrase, *Responsibility Deficit Disorder* (RDD). Sapadin says that, "RDD is prevalent in our society and is a growing problem." You can contribute to RDD in your workplace if you make certain that the question "who will answer for the team's work?" goes unanswered. Since team members tend to do as their leader, make sure that you never take personal responsibility for your behavior, your decisions, or your performance. The buck *does not* stop with you!

Additionally, don't expect team members to act responsibly, and don't insist on it. Allow the team to do their own thing and signal your approval by never calling them on their behavior. Never inspect or expect your team's results.

Leave them to their own devices, and offer excuses to your boss when asked about their progress.

Do all within your power to demolish the notion of interdependence. The last thing you want is for your team members to believe is that they can be much more successful by learning to coordinate their efforts. In fact, whenever you see your members trying to work together and help each other, squash it! Also, disregard all formal evaluation processes, that way you won't be tempted to evaluate the team or its individual members.

THE TEAM MEMBER'S MISTAKE:
Unaccountable and Unresponsive

If it is true that if one person fails the whole team fails, then your success as a leader depends on total accountability from your team. Women leaders have to have 20/20 vision to distinguish unaccountable team members from responsible ones. Who are they?

- They are lone wolves.
- They don't meet deadlines.
- They shirk responsibility.
- They create excuses and cover up the truth in regards to assignments.

Here's an example of one such excuse:

Q. Did you create the spreadsheet I needed?

A. Oh, my computer was down all afternoon and the I.T. guys are on vacation.

Translation: I didn't do it, and I'm not going to do it. You're better off assigning it to someone else. Go away and leave me alone!

HOW TO AVOID THIS MISTAKE:
Can I Count on You?

Accountability and responsibility must be focal points of your leadership. Do not feel uncomfortable or embarrassed to approach your team members about poor performance; if you don't, it will affect the team. Use these techniques to stop it before it starts:

- Make sure your team knows they can always reach out for help. This lets them know that if they do get stuck or have problems you are there.
- Make and enforce deadlines. Deadlines add pressure, but also create accountability.
- Give your team members the authority to make decisions. This will help to develop competence and confidence.
- Once you have done everything in your power to create an atmosphere of accountability, your options

become limited: One rotten apple spoils the bunch. Get rid of the rotten apple!

LEAD LIKE A WOMAN
Use Your Executive Social Skills

In this section, I want to share two words of advice. First, if you must be someone, be yourself! Let's kill the myth that women leaders have to act like men to be successful. As women take on more leadership roles in the workplace, many believe they have to emulate the leadership style of their male counterparts—barking orders, being mean and gruff, etc. Nothing could be further from the truth. Be your authentic self and not a female version of your male boss—former, current, or future.

Women have natural abilities that can prove to be advantageous within their organizations and within their teams. In fact, according to Dr. Fisher, "Women have what scientists call 'executive social skills.'" For example, women (generally speaking) encourage involvement. Just think back to our political system and the strides we've made as a nation as they relate to dealing with the injustices women have endured.

Susan B. Anthony embodied the authenticity principle. She was unafraid to speak *her* mind. Notice I italicized *her* to emphasize that during Susan's era a woman was not encouraged nor expected to think or speak for herself! Yet, Anthony did what comes naturally and encouraged women to get involved in the process so that the process could be changed. According to her website:

> In 1868 Anthony encouraged working women from the printing and sewing trades in New York, who were excluded from men's trade unions, to form Workingwomen's Associations. As a delegate to the National Labor Congress in 1868 Anthony persuaded the committee on female labor to call for votes for women and equal pay for equal work, although the men at the conference deleted the reference to the vote.

Success is merely a by-product of authenticity. Psychologists at RHR International conducted a study of women leaders and concluded:

> "When a woman is operating at her most authentic self, she simultaneously feels and is viewed as being a more effective leader. She is a catalyst for meaningful and positive change; a high-performing, confident individual; and a critical player in the organization's overall success."

Second, if you mess up, fess up! No one is perfect—not *even* you or me! Everyone makes mistakes. Sometimes we (women leaders) are hesitant to admit a mistake because we're afraid of being seen as less competent than our male counterparts. When I was working on my master's degree in Organizational Leadership, I had to read *The Leadership Challenge* authored by James M. Kouzes and Barry Z. Posner. Kouzes and Posner said, "Apologies need to be genuine to be believable . . . it's important to quickly own up to it [your mistake] to maintain your credibility." The most trusted leaders are those who own up to their mistakes and willingly share their faux pas with their team members.

Lead like a woman and be your authentic self rather than mimic your male counterparts. Use your executive social skills to encourage involvement and accountability on your team. Additionally, because of the natural executive social skills you possess, remember are personally endowed with the ability to hold yourself and your team accountable—it's the only way you can succeed.

LEADERSHIP SELF-ASSESSMENT

How do you measure up? Use this page to objectively assess yourself and your team. Download your Leadership Assessment Guide at: kbpbjz.bookhip.com

It's All About Freedom

There was a woman who had been a manager of a successful hotel for years. Systematically over time, the rooms in the hotel were remodeled. It had been customary every fall for Jan, the hotel's owner, to redo at least four rooms. She chose to do the renovations in the fall so she could maximize tourism in the summer.

With the end of summer came the start of fall, and once again it was time for renovations. However, this time around Jan did not see the renovations able to be carried out in a timely manner. Her workload had increased. She doubted if she could renovate the rooms to perfection like she always did.

What about her staff? They hated placing guests in the rooms in need of renovation. In the staff's eyes those rooms were not up to standard, and offered the customers poor value. Armed with this knowledge and realizing her predicament Jan formed an idea. It was time to empower her staff. She assigned each staff member a room for them to renovate. She allowed them the freedom to do this with very little interruption from her. When the summer months came around the rooms were completed.

Now the staff had no problems placing guests in the rooms, and could be heard telling them, "You're sleeping in my room tonight!"

Here's the point: When you empower employees you create a connection to the organization, and an avenue for increased production. Remember, "You're sleeping in my room tonight!"

THE LEADER'S MISTAKE:
Become Megan the Micro-manager

This step is extremely easy! All you have to do is be a control freak, a micro-manager; you know the kind of manager that will not allow your team the freedom necessary to accomplish its goals. Be the stereotypical overbearing mom that controls every facet of the household.

Just follow this checklist and you can audition for and win the role of Megan the micro-manager:

- Insist that they check in with you every step of the way.

- Always confuse measuring with monitoring; monitor everything and over measure the rest!
- Brow beat them into doing everything your way.
- Give them no freedom to learn or grow. Think of this mistake as empowerment in reverse. Oh, there's a word for that, *disempowerment.*
- Talk about how you empower your team members, but never do it. You can best make this mistake if you make sure your team knows that you don't trust their decision-making abilities.
- Cripple them so that they feel uncomfortable taking the initiative, and if you have a few misfits on the team, who dare to work independently of your input, stop them dead in their tracks! After all, it is essential that everyone knows that you are in control and they have no power!
- Insist on being kept "in the loop" on everything— no matter how minor.
- Correct team members in front of others.
- Take the "just to clarify" stance and restate a team member's message in different words. For example, if Kristie sends out an email that says, "We're meeting in the Executive Board room at 11. Please bring your case studies," immediately send an email that says, "Just to clarify, all the members of the team will be meeting. Please bring your drafts of the case study."

- Make every project a priority. This will drive your team members crazy and will allow you to stand over them to "keep all the balls in the air."

THE TEAM MEMBER'S MISTAKE:
Mutiny on the Bounty

I realize that what you're about to read may cause you some discomfort. However, remember that someone is after your spot. Yes, there's probably at least one person on your team who has decided that he or she can do a much better job than you. So what does your nemesis look like?

- She is always critical of leadership—yours, your boss, and everyone else in the organization.
- She usually voices her criticisms in front of team members and upper management.
- She talks behind your back and accuses you of "empowerment" as a way to shirk responsibility.
- She openly shows her dissatisfaction with the performance of "empowered" team members.
- When she is "empowered" she keeps the power in her hands only.
- She openly disrespects you.
- She feels ignored and seeks attention, even if the attention is negative.

HOW TO AVOID THIS MISTAKE:
Embrace the Fairy Tale

Follow the Goldilocks formula when it comes to empowering your team—not too little, not too much, but just enough.

Make sure you are judicious in sharing power. Always measure the doses of power given to your team members. Give them too much power and you have to concern yourself with ambitions for your job. Give them too little and you stand a chance of creating dependents. When you do share power, use it as a vote of confidence.

Additionally, follow the five steps Nicole Vulcan outlines in her article, *How to Deal With an Employee Who is Trying to Sabotage You:*

1. *Develop a workplace code of conduct, and put it in your employee handbook. By clearly outlining the behaviors that are accepted and not accepted in the workplace, you'll have something to refer to when an employee gets out of line. Your code of conduct code may include directions about what employees can and cannot reveal about the company in social media and other outside outlets, how they deal with the press, and how employees are expected to treat one another. Make all employees aware that you've created this code of conduct; or if you already have one, send it out as a reminder.*

2. *Open up the lines of communication. If you have one employee who's trying to sabotage you, chances are she has some complaints—and she may not be the only one. Allow the employee to sound off about her complaints in a group setting, such as a regularly scheduled team meeting in which all staff are invited to make suggestions for improving the workplace. During these meetings, be very careful in your language and communication materials, taking steps to show workers that you want their voices to be heard. When you hear feedback, work on implementing the suggested changes, and then report back about your progress at the next meeting.*

3. *Document any instances of sabotage you observe. If you already know the employee is trying to sabotage you, chances are it's because you've seen or heard about things she's doing to bring you down. Write down the date, time and nature of the incidents, and keep them in a safe place where co-workers will not stumble upon them. In the event that the problem escalates and the employee tries to get you fired -- or tries to destroy the reputation of the company -- you'll have evidence of her directed efforts against you, which may prove she's more vindictive than victim.*

4. *Arrange a one-on-one meeting with the employee to discuss the issues she may be having. Sometimes, simply talking about the issues may help you discover what it is about you that the employee doesn't like. This may involve developing an action plan for both you and her to follow, so that you're both engaging in behaviors that are amenable to both parties. By remaining humble and lis-*

tening to what she has to say, you may be able to come to some compromise that has her feeling listened to and understood, while at the same time leaving you feeling more secure about the future. At the same time, remember that you're the boss; so remain the authority and don't let her dictate all the terms. After the meeting, document the content of the conversation.

5. *Talk with your Human Resources department or your direct supervisor about the problem. If things are getting out of hand and you've made an attempt to solve the issue yourself, you need to get others involved. Your HR department or fellow managers can help you monitor the situation and keep an eye out for bad behavior; they can also provide direction about a possible reassignment of duties for the person, or possibly even advise that you let the person go.*

LEAD LIKE A WOMAN
Strategic Empowerment

Women are wired for inclusion, defined by Merriam-Webster as "the act of including." I've been blessed with two granddaughters, ages two and four. Their five cousins are all boys ranging in ages from eighteen down to one year. I've noticed that my granddaughters are more inclined to insist that the other children play together; whereas, my grandsons are more inclined to play alone. I'm certainly not offering this as scientific proof; however, I believe it does support the premise that females are generally predisposed to a more interpersonal style of communication.

Sally Helgesen published *The Female Advantage* in 1990. Her fascinating work in the area of women in leadership has become a leadership classic. Helgesen coined a phrase "The Web of Influence" which was a systematic portrayal of how women bring a type of leadership that differs from traditional, masculine and military hierarchical systems of leadership. Ms. Helgesen observed that women leaders demonstrate "collaborative, courageous, flexible, open, accessible relationships." Because women leaders create open accessible relationships, they possess the inherent ability to include, support, and empower their team members.

Let me ask you: What is your definition of empowerment? If you have no definition or don't understand the word, how can you put it to use? You can't *just do it* if you don't know what *it* means. The simplest definition of empower is to enable, and your goal is to enable your team members to act. Enabling them to act does not mean relinquishing your power; rather, it means giving it away strategically.

Strategy 1: Determine reasonable benchmarks for each project and ignore everything else. The benefit to this strategy is that it empowers you to work on other projects while empowering your team members to get their jobs done with a specific target in mind.

Strategy 2: Make sure your team members know that you are available to monitor their efforts and coach their performance *if and when* they feel they need your help.

Strategy 3: Respect your team's time and make decisions that affect them sooner and not later. In other words, don't be the bottleneck!

Strategy 4: Let your team make mistakes so that they can develop stronger skills. Mistakes are often a catalyst for growth.

Can you ride a bike? I bet you can. Do you remember how you learned? You kept falling down until you got the hang of maintaining your balance. There's something innate in most women that causes us to want to protect people. We don't want the child to fall. Listen, great women leaders understand that they can't jump in all the time to fix things. Please don't misinterpret what I just said. It's okay to provide guidance—just like it was okay for your mom, dad, or a sibling to hold the back of the bike while you were learning how to ride it. You needed a little help. To continue with the metaphor, don't hold the bike forever. If you have team members that don't learn from their mistakes, you need to remove them from the team.

Lead like a woman and empower your team members to act. Remember, as a woman, you possess the innate ability to encourage participation and involvement—it's in your DNA.

LEADERSHIP SELF-ASSESSMENT

How do you measure up? Use this page to objectively assess yourself and your team. Download your Leadership Assessment Guide at: kbpbiz.bookhip.com

Make Sure They Die on the Vine

A thief was caught after stealing some paintings from the Louvre in Paris, when his getaway van ran out of fuel.

Given bail at his first hearing, a reporter asked him on the steps of the courthouse how he forgot such a vital part of his plan.

"Simple," said the thief, "I had no Monet for Degas to make the Van Gogh."

I know that was a corny joke, but the purpose of this joke is to emphasize what a lack of resources can do to a winning plan. If the thief would have given his driver the resources to fuel the van, then he would not have gotten caught.

THE LEADER'S MISTAKE:
Starve Them and Stunt Their Growth

I must confess: this is my favorite chapter! You may recall that I am an international conference speaker and corporate trainer, and I see this mistake all too often: leaders who do not understand the value of lifelong learning.

Let's break this gaffe down into bit-sized pieces to help you accelerate the destruction of your team. It's simple—just let them die on the vine, and here's your checklist to make sure that you know exactly what to do:

- Offer no training—online, off-site, on-site—no training!
- Refuse to pay for training if they ask for it.
- Discourage them from finding mentors.
- Tell them only losers go back to college—after all, everything they need to know about succeeding they probably learned in kindergarten!
- Give in to your natural inclination to hunker down in these slow economic times. I mean, everyone knows the first two things you cut in a down economy are travel and training, right?
- Repeat after me: "Training is expensive. Our company is too small for that! Besides, our employees know how to do their jobs; what's there to train?"

- The next time one of the team members comes to you asking for training, just tell them be grateful they have a job. That will make them feel lousy!

THE TEAM MEMBER'S MISTAKE:
"Ain't Nobody Got Time for That!"

I met Charlotte (not her real name) in an Administrative Assistants Conference I conducted in the Midwest. Charlotte told me she had been in her position for more than 25 years and the conference was her first-ever training. She then went on to explain to me that she had a new boss, and if that boss wanted to waste money sending Charlotte to *this*—fine by her. Yes, she actually referred to my conference as *this* with a distinctive sound of distain. Charlotte was not motivated and it was a day-long challenge to keep her negative energy at bay. The problem is, though, you have a Charlotte on your team and she's spewing venom every chance she gets. Here's what the Charlottes on the team do:

- They just want to maintain the status quo.
- They hate taking new training classes and attending seminars.
- They douse team member's excitement about learning something new.
- They bad mouth new training programs and methods.
- They refuse to learn anything new.

- They say things like, "I don't know why I have to go to that stupid training. It has nothing to do with me or my job!"
- They tell me (the trainer) that you (their boss) are the one that should be in my class because you're the one with the problem!

HOW TO AVOID THIS MISTAKE:
Protect Your Investment

The smartest women leaders realize that the only way for their organization to grow is if the individuals within the organization grow. As far back as the 1930's experts have advised that knowledge is a determining factor for economic growth. Please . . . read the latter part of that sentence again!

Savvy business women also realize that each employee represents an investment, and they look for ways to protect that investment. They're always looking for meaningful ways to provide professional development opportunities for their team members, and preferably ways that will yield a return on their investment. They find ways to afford development, even when there is "not enough money for that."

Further, they help their members work toward achieving professional goals. For example, if they notice a team member needs better communication skills, they're always on the lookout for chances and classes to help that team member develop that skill.

LEAD LIKE A WOMAN
Use Your People Skills

Did you know that "people skills" are associated with the female hormone, estrogen? People skills are "a set of skills enabling a person to get along with others, to communicate ideas effectively, to resolve conflicts, and to achieve personal or business goals. People skills are essential for business functions..." One of the most important people skills is your ability to achieve your business goals by providing motivation and training to your team.

I cannot tell you how many people have attended one of my seminars, conferences, or break-out sessions and made it painfully obvious they were a prisoner. Speakers and trainers worldwide, including me, define a prisoner as someone who was sent for training as a disciplinary action. It's the leader's last-ditch effort to make Jason behave and do his job. Well, here's the problem with that tactic, Jason has no intrinsic motivation *or* you don't know what motivates him.

As an excellent leader, it is important to do constant motivation checks on your team. When you perform regular motivation checks, you can understand what motivates your team. You can also see which team members are the most motivated. I agree with Chris Young of the *Rainmaker Group* who advises that "not everyone is motivated by the same thing." Young had identified six major types of motivators listed below. Use Young's list to help you assess motivation on a team member by team member basis.

*1. **Utilitarian***: *motivation for money as well as efficiency. People high in this particular value are more "careful" with how they spend their time, energy, and may want to make more money. $1000 in cash may motivate.*

*2. **Knowledge:** motivation to learn, to understand the "truth" about something. People with a high knowledge "factor" may want to spend more time learning. The reward may be to actually send them to additional learning opportunities as a reward. Literally a reward for learning and completing a test may be additional learning. A $1000 learning program may motivate.*

*3. **Social:** motivation to help others. A proper reward for someone with a high Social motivator may be to give them a day off to give back to the community. A $1000 donated to a desired cause may motivate.*

*4. **Aesthetic:** motivation for nice things, surroundings, clothing, life-fulfillment. A reward for someone with a high Aesthetic may be to give them a pass to an art gallery, a gift certificate to a high-end clothing store, a home-decorating gift card, or a pass to bungee jumping. A $1000 membership to several museums may motivate.*

*5. **Power:** motivation to control one's own destiny as well as the destiny of others. A way to motivate someone with a higher power motivation is to let them lead a project, lead others, or perhaps a gift certificate for professional career* *planning. A $1000 investment in leadership development may motivate.*

6. Tradition: *motivation to live one's life according to a set standard. Depending upon one's beliefs, a person may be motivated by their specific belief system and any type of respect of or recognition of this belief system. A $1000 donation to someone's belief system may motivate.*

In Jason's case knowledge is *not* his motivator, so you're wasting valuable time and money sending him to training. This clearly suggests that training is not always the right answer. David Kelly, the director of training at Carver Federal Savings Bank puts it this way:

"For some organizations, delivering training is the go-to solution for just about any new problem . . . .

Unfortunately, workers in many cases have learned that despite their company's investment in training, their job performance isn't likely to improve as a result of new training —that training often isn't the right solution. We need to learn that lesson for ourselves, and start adding other performance support tools to our portfolio, and use training only in situations where it's appropriate."

You may not want to hear this; however, you might need to relieve Jason of his duties. That's a nice way of saying, "fire him!"

Seek out as many professional development opportunities for your team as possible. Consider paying for it yourself if your company won't. Why? Because once your team gains a new skill, it's theirs; no one can take it from them.

When you do invest in professional development, look for companies that are willing to guarantee a return on your investment. Remember this:

> *"The old paradigm for development tacitly assumes change occurs dramatically and immediately. Send people through a two-day seminar, and—voilà—they are transformed. As a result of this misguided assumption, people are sent through brief trainings that have little lasting effect . . . A single seminar or workshop is a beginning, but it is not sufficient in itself . . . Reaching the point where a new habit replaces the old takes extensive practice."* Daniel Goleman

One of the best and sometimes most overlooked ways to achieve personal and professional success is through lifelong learning.

Lead like a woman and use your people skills to make investing in your team's professional and personal development a priority to guarantee achieving your business goals.

LEADERSHIP SELF-ASSESSMENT

How do you measure up? Use this page to objectively assess yourself and your team. Download your Leadership Assessment Guide at: kbpbjz.bookhip.com

You Can Trust Me . . . *Really*!

O n an intense Wednesday morning Jill and her assistant prepared themselves for the meeting. If all went well Jill's department could be positioned for upward movement within the organization.

Of course, all went well. Maybe well is too small of an adjective. All went magnificent. Jill's presentation impressed upper management. As a matter of fact, because of her presentation they offered Jill another position. The formula that she had created . . . well not her, but her assistant Carla had created—this formula was her ticket to the top.

Kevin from headquarters was fascinated with her ideas and promised her that this formula would be the fuel that would explode her career!

She glanced nervously at Carla whose pleading eyes seemed to say, "Jill, don't forget to mention my name. Please don't forget to give me credit for my contribution." Jan chose to ignore Carla's pleading look and took all of the credit for herself. Why did she have to give Carla any credit? Jill was the leader. She reasoned that if she looked good her team would look good. Jill's silence in not mentioning Carla was purposeful. Carla would get over it. Besides, the team was going to prosper from her success anyway.

You know what they say about karma . . . Ten years later Carla had moved up in the company. As fate would have it she had advanced past Jill. In an unanticipated turn of events Carla had to fire Jill. You see, Jill had not learned her lesson about taking credit for someone else's work. It caused her bosses to realize if Jill's team couldn't trust her, then maybe they couldn't either.

THE LEADER'S MISTAKE:
Be the Boss Who Can't be Trusted

Do you want to inspire distrust and a general lack of faith in your leadership? Take note from this extensive list:

- Make a promise to your team and don't keep it. Tell them you, your boss, and for that matter everyone above you can't be held accountable for *every* promise made, because integrity is not the strong suit of management and hey, *stuff happens*!

- Make sure you let your team know it is all about the bottom line with you. Through a series of underhanded, cut-throat, and uncaring actions you will be able to drive home this point.
- If at all possible dismiss words like "value," "ethics," and "morals" because these words are positive words associated with trust. You are doing the opposite.
- Throw team members under the bus every chance you get.
- Be a bona fide backstabber. Talk behind your team members' backs and make sure they know that's what you do.
- Lie to your boss to cover up mistakes and keep your boss in the dark as much as possible.
- Be a "yes" woman. Refuse to stand up for your team and let them fend for themselves.

THE TEAM MEMBER'S MISTAKE:
It's All About Me

It probably comes as no surprise that the untrustworthy team member's list mirrors the untrustworthy leader's list. In fact, the untrustworthy team member was blindly promoted to her position of leadership. But you know how the saying goes, right? "Once a snake . . . always a snake." So as to save you the trouble of turning back a page, I'll just rinse, repeat, and add to their list! Team members that exhibit these tendencies should make any leader say "hmm . . ."

- They make promises and don't keep them.
- They throw you and fellow team members under the bus every chance they get.
- They are bona fide backstabbers. They talk behind fellow team members' backs.
- They lie to you to cover up their mistakes and keep you in the dark as much as possible.
- They agree to everything on the surface, but have no loyalty to you or the team.
- They refuse to acknowledge or gain from fellow team members' knowledge, experiences, and skills.
- They criticize any new idea, and never offer assistance.
- They throw office tantrums and hold grudges whenever they don't get their way.
- They seem especially suspicious of management's intentions.

HOW TO AVOID THIS MISTAKE:
Set an Example

It's said if one wants trust, one must first be trustworthy. Your team has to trust you if you want to build a foundation to trust them. The most effective leaders understand this concept and how to incite this feeling in their team.

Here are some great examples of how to form a reciprocal trust relationship with your team.

- Start with yourself; create a personal creed that embodies your personal values and beliefs and governs how you behave. This will help you to make decisions that both you and your team feel good about—even when things don't go as planned.
- Educate your team; give them the tools it takes to be competent in their position. Make sure they know their stuff. When team members can count on each other to get their part of the job done, their "trust" stakes go up.
- Periodically assign a team member to be the team troubleshooter, this lets the team know they can depend on each other, and in turn it instills confidence in the person.
- Make this your team's motto, "Our word is our bond." When you create an atmosphere of team accountability it manifest into personal accountability. Reliability goes a long way in creating trust. When your team knows they can count on you, you will be able to count on them, too.

LEAD LIKE A WOMAN
Embrace the Transformational You

In a 2013 Research Symposium Dr. Alice Eagly, an expert on gender and leadership, updated her work on women as leaders. Here's what Dr. Eagly said about women and ethics, "Meta-analyses of studies on ethical beliefs and decision-making have shown that women are more likely than men to support ethical business practices." Ethics are simply the moral principles that govern a person's or a group's behavior. While I realize I'm painting with a broad stroke here, if women are more likely to support ethical business practices then they have to be women who have personal morals and ethics.

Eagly conducted an earlier study with colleagues, and their meta-analysis from that study "showed that female managers are somewhat more transformational than male managers."

While working on my graduate degree, I was introduced to several different leadership models. I won't take the time to explain all of them. I will, however, explain the Transformational Leadership model to which Dr. Eagly refers.

James McGregor Burns introduced the transformational leadership model in his 1978 book, *Leadership*. This approach to leadership emphasizes ways to "elevate leaders and followers to higher levels of morality and motivation."

Further research into transformational leaders identified five primary characteristics, one of which is integrity.

Leaders with integrity follow through, practice what they preach, and walk the talk. In contrast, leaders who lack integrity provide no basis for followers to infer actions from their words. I dare not suggest that integrity is a trait unique to women. Clearly, those in leadership—be they women or men—can be sorely lacking in the integrity department. However, according to clinical psychologist Dr. Seth Myers, integrity is a behavior that can be cultivated.

> *The good news about integrity is that we're not born with it—or without it—which means that it's a behavior-based virtue we can cultivate over time. We can set a goal to show more integrity in everyday life..."*

Effective leaders know the importance of creating a trusting, cooperative atmosphere because they know that's what it takes to build effective teams. The key word in the previous sentence is the root word of "trusting" which as you know is "trust." Trust allows you to keep the lines of communication open.

Leadership expert, Warren Bennis says, "Leadership without mutual trust is a contradiction in terms . . . " The people who work for you must believe in you. They must trust themselves and each other. Further, they must believe that as a team they can rise to any challenge.

Lead like a woman and remember that leadership experts have found that you are somewhat more transformational in your leadership style than a man. Learn to be your transformational self and show your team that morals and ethics are important to you. Show them that you will always be ethical in your dealings with them.

Know this: once trust is gone, it's gone; so do all you can to preserve it! And keep this in mind: "A leader with integrity has one self, at home and at work, with family and with colleagues. Leaders without integrity are putting on an act."

LEADERSHIP SELF-ASSESSMENT

How do you measure up? Use this page to objectively assess yourself and your team. Download your Leadership Assessment Guide at: kbpbjz.bookhip.com

No Creativity Allowed

Many years ago two salesmen were sent by a British shoe manufacturer to Africa to investigate and report back on market potential.

The first salesman reported back, "There is no potential here—nobody wears shoes."

The second salesman reported back, "There is massive potential here—nobody wears shoes."

The background: Shoe Company International had a seminar in the fall of 1967. It had been required training for all of upper management. Unfortunately, Don had a family emergency and missed the seminar. His team of salesmen where the only salesmen in the company who didn't get a chance to benefit from what was supposed to be new sales training. Salesman number two was from Don's team.

Okay. I embellished the story a bit! But you get my point, don't you? If "creativity is just connecting things," as Steve Jobs once said, then creativity in its purest form is finding a solution to a challenge.

THE LEADER'S MISTAKE:
Turn Out the Lights

According to business experts from liveplan.com, "The most successful organizations have come to realize that it is creativity that drives innovation and creates the type of working environment that lures and retains employees." If you want to avoid building the kind of team that makes people want to join and stay, just follow these strategies:

- Never let them flip the switch of creativity on. Whenever the Eureka light bulb goes off in team members quickly dim it.
- Insist that team members focus on the problem. Whenever they talk about a solution, refocus their attention to the gaps and imperfections inherent in their proposed solution.
- Discourage solution-oriented thinking, and be on the constant lookout for trouble. After you find it, make sure you let the team know that mistakes are not tolerated on your team.

- Tell them you are not interested in their research and to stop daydreaming and get some real work done!
- Tell them you have no time to invest in their "hairbrained" ideas because creativity on your team is simply not allowed!

THE TEAM MEMBER'S MISTAKE:
Sticks and Stones, but Words . . .

Is there any office in the country that doesn't have name callers? You know—those team members that love to belittle and dismiss everyone else's ideas. The "Oh, that is a stupid idea!" girl, and the "How is that idea even relevant?" guy. Those team members are experts at destroying others' ability to create. How do you identify them?

- They criticize team members who dare to think differently.
- They criticize creative thinking as daydreaming and demand "real work" be done.
- They belittle and dismiss other team members' ideas.
- They always focus on the problem and never the solution.
- They never display any substantive amount of curiousity.

- They are afraid to take risks and discourage other team members who dare try.
- They show little passion for their job.

HOW TO AVOID THIS MISTAKE:
Think Outside the Box . . . Heck, Just Get Rid of It!

Have you ever visited the Pinterest website? Who hasn't, right? Did you know that its visual layout was modeled after cofounder Ben Silbermann's many different collections? In an interview with *Hutch* founder Chris Dixon, Silbermann explained Pinterest this way:

> *"As a child, Silbermann enjoyed collecting things, from insects to stamps. 'What you collect says so much about who you are,' he mused. Pinterest was built to help people continue their collections online."*

I mention this because it demonstrates what happens when people allow their creative juices to flow. I also want you to rethink how much or how little creativity is actually flowing on your team.

Creativity fosters problem solving, and a good leader knows that. Here's a list of five tips that I often share in my *Women's Leadership Conferences* to encourage a team's creativity:

1. ***Encourage them—"if you like it, I love it!"*** My mom would say that to me every time I came to her with one of my ideas…no matter how weird it sounded. Once I told her I wanted to create a mop/broom gadget that would suck up cobwebs with little effort from the person using it. That was my answer to our weekly house cleaning routine! If she thought it was a horrible idea, she never let on. Mom was wise enough to know that I needed to know the importance of creativity and that I needed validation. Your team is no different!

   Make sure they know that you will listen to their ideas. Help them understand that thinking outside the box—even getting rid of the box—is how they can contribute to a company that stands above the rest.

2. ***Start gamestorming.*** Years ago the buzz word for generating ideas was *brainstorming*. Merriam-Webster defines brainstorming this way: "a group problem-solving technique that involves the spontaneous contribution of ideas from all members of the group; *also*: the mulling over of ideas by one or more individuals in an attempt to devise or find a solution to a problem." Brainstorming has its place; however, I suggest you kick it up a notch and start gamestorming.

   Gamestorming, according to Pete Sena, "is idea generation through a structured play activity, such as short games and exercises." Sena, a gamestorming expert, explains, "Gamestorming works by drawing boundaries—like kids playing wiffle ball deciding the doghouse will be first base and a stack of firewood will be second base. When we understand the "ground rules," we are freed to play—and even compete—in ways that make sense. You never see social loafing and sucker effects in wiffle ball, do you?

You know it's a great gamestorm when you can't tell the boss from the intern. Everyone is only focused on solving a problem. Egos are gone, titles are gone, and along with it, all constraints our society creates that aren't helpful to innovation."

Before you look with distain at the idea of gamestorming, remember this: Adults love to play games! Consider the fact that the game *Pokemon Go*, was reportedly downloaded 15 million times after Nintendo released it in July, 2016. Vox.com reported that, "More than 40 percent of the adults who downloaded the mobile app are older than 25, and about one in three adult users are women." Pokemon aside, as of this writing, 155 million Americans spend three or more hours each week playing games, and the average gamer is 35.

Harness your employees energy and creativity, and join the ranks of companies like Google, Apple, Facebook—all use gamestorming. Sena sums it up nicely, "Rather than seeing innovation as an errand, they look at it as a way of driving culture and getting results. And it's this type of thinking that's going to build a creative workforce and an innovation culture."

3. *Routinely ask your staff to share their ideas with you and the rest of the team.* I learned the value of this idea from my employment with IBM. There were suggestion boxes placed strategically around our department. I made a suggestion on a way to cut down on how we monitored a customer's equipment once it left our warehouse. My reward? $2,000! Back then one of my motivators was money!

One of my industry colleagues, Alexander Kjerulf, has suggested getting rid of the suggestion box and replacing it with a suggestion flowchart—something he saw during one of his visits to Cape Town, Johannesburg. You can visit his website to see what it looks like: http://positivesharing.com/2014/02/kill-suggestion-box-heres-much-better-way/

Here's how it works:

1. *The first step is to post your idea to a board that hangs in a prominent spot in the office and get 12 of your coworkers to also sign on. If you like an idea, you show your support in a very low-tech way: you put a sticker on it.*

2. *Some ideas die at this stage—there's just not enough energy or support behind the proposal. All*

ideas that don't make it for one reason or another are displayed in The Graveyard.

3. Here you can see each idea that failed and why. If an idea does get the necessary support, the person behind it writes a one-page proposal which is then submitted to Quirk's EXCO, which is basically their top leadership team. If they approve it, the idea goes ahead immediately and is placed on the "Ideas in motion" section of the board.

4. Ideas that were previously approved are shown on the "It's happening" section.

5. Of course, the leadership group can turn the idea down, and if they do, they must carefully explain why they don't think it's a good idea. They can't just say "No" or "Maybe later." Even if the leadership group turns an idea down, that need not be the end of it. If a person feels that this idea is still too good to ignore, it can be put to a debate and subsequent vote inside the company. If the idea is voted through, this overrides the EXCO's decision and the idea goes ahead anyway.

6. Another thing they do on the board is highlight the costs of previous ideas, so employees know how much things end up costing.

4. ***Research and keep up with your industry's best practices***. Creativity feeds innovation, and innovation is what your company needs to remain cutting edge. When

your team knows what's going on their industry, they help to position your company to be ahead of potential mistakes and missteps. Consider Amazon.co.uk., for example, a company that started out as just an online book retailer in 1998. Sophie Curtis, a writer with Business Insider, writes that by 2013 Amazon expanded to offering their "customers more than 100 million items in over 30 product categories, ranging from health and beauty to sportswear and groceries." To what did they credit their phenomenal growth? Innovation!

In fact, Xavier Garambois, Vice President of EU Retail put it this way, "Innovation is part of the Amazon DNA and over the past 15 years we have been constantly adding and refining technology that enhances and improves the experience of all our customers."

Remember what I told you, creativity feeds innovation, so make sure your team knows what's going on in your company's industry.

5. *Accept imperfection.* Creative thinkers are willing to take risks and sometimes those risks don't pan out. As the leader, you have to be willing to accept this fact, and continue to encourage your team to think creatively. I'm a pretty good Poker player; however, I wouldn't be if I weren't willing to take a risk and yes—lose more than I win. When I play Poker, I have to pay attention to the other players to determine their tells—what they

do when they're bluffing, etc. Sometimes I get it right. Sometimes I get it wrong. You'll see the same pattern with your team. I'll sum up my advice in three simple steps:

- Know they will make mistakes.
- Let them learn from their mistakes.
- Be okay with the process.

Encourage your employees to look for solutions to your teams' challenges outside the norm. Give them the freedom to experiment and to make mistakes. Creativity sanctioned and unleashed through the leader positions your team not merely for survival, but more importantly, growth.

When it comes to understanding the need for creativity, you have to be smarter than the naysayers on your team. Involve them in different ways to resolve team challenges, and encourage them to share the options with the rest of the team. When these team members dismiss and belittle someone else's ideas, ask them how could they improve the idea or do they have an idea. Periodically place the name callers in "what if" scenarios. This will help you and your team focus on solutions.

It is said that, "creativity is a medium for success." Any serious businesswoman with aspirations has fully grasped this concept.

LEAD LIKE A WOMAN
Nurture, Don't Mother!

Here's some interesting research albeit old, but interesting nonetheless:

> *"Moskal (1997) summarizes findings from a study conducted since 1988 by the Foundation of Future Leadership. The study involved evaluations of effectiveness for more than 900 managers at major corporations. They found that "women's effectiveness as managers, leaders, and teammates outstrips the abilities of their male counterparts in 28 of 31 managerial skill areas—including the challenging areas of meeting deadlines, keeping productivity high, and **generating new ideas**.*

> *These are impressive results, especially considering that over 70% of the individuals involved in the assessment process were male. Also of interest was that women consistently rated themselves lower than their male counterparts in each of the skill areas."*

What is generating new ideas if it's not creativity? And how can you, a woman in leadership, cultivate a culture of creativity on your team? The word that comes to mind is *nurture* not to be confused with mother.

Much of the research on women in leadership roles suggest that women are successful because of they naturally possess greater nurturing skills. A 2014 study published by leadership consultancy Zenger Folkman found that female leaders do, in fact, carry a slight edge over their male counterparts in the nurturing skills department. That's the good news.

The bad news is that the same quality that can make you a great leader is the same quality that can make you a poor leader. I know I've said it once, but it bears repeating: don't confuse nurturing with mothering! Your team members are not your children; consequently, they do not require you to coddle or babysit them to encourage their creativity.

Lead like a woman and tap into your natural ability to support your team's creative efforts and help them develop their ideas. Afterall, research has proven that you are well-equipped to help others generate ideas. Further, you naturally possess the kinds of nuturing skills that you should use to to help your team keep your organization out front and successful.

LEADERSHIP SELF-ASSESSMENT

How do you measure up? Use this page to objectively assess yourself and your team. Download your Leadership Assessment Guide at: kbpbjz.bookhip.com

We've Never Done it Like That Before

D o you remember Blockbuster, the video store? Years ago, Blockbuster was *the* place to rent the latest movies and game . . . that is until Netflix and streaming video came along.

Blockbuster L.L.C. was an American-based provider of home video and video game rental services. At its peak in 2004, Blockbuster had up to 60,000 employees and over 9,000 stores. Because of competition from other video rental companies such as Netflix, Blockbuster lost significant revenue, and filed for bankruptcy on September 23, 2010, and again on April 6, 2011.

What happened? How did Blockbuster go from having a strangle hold on the home video market to going bankrupt twice? Is it possible that from the executives down to the lowest employee, change was never considered or was stubbornly resisted?

THE LEADER'S MISTAKE:
"That's Not How We Do It!"

When women leaders fail to recognize change, or that change is needed, failure is close behind. Do you want to continue to always be one step behind your industry's leaders? Do you want your team constantly and consistently underperforming? Do you want to miss out on opportunities that could further your career? If so, make sure that you avoid change as a leader, change in your team, and change in general. The next time change is suggested—be it from a team member or your boss, just say:

- "We have never done it like that before."
- "That will never work."
- "We've already tried it, and it got us nowhere."
- "That's the way we've always done it, and that's the way we're going to continue to do it!"
- "No one is going to go for that!"
- "That's too risky, and there's no guarantee of success."
- "Why change? Things are fine just the way they are."
- "That's going to be too hard for us to do."

If you are looking for a way to reject change, follow the steps listed above.

THE TEAM MEMBER'S MISTAKES:
Old Dogs...No Tricks!

Women leaders who have aspirations to reach the top rung on the corporate ladder know that when it comes to managing people you have to create an army of team members that ask the question, "Where's my change?" It is important that your team understand that they are chameleons. Adaptability and adjustment have to be ingrained in them. However, there are team members who just can't accept change. Who are they? They're the ones who say things like:

- "We've never done it like that before."
- "That will never work."
- "We've already tried it, and it got us nowhere."
- "That's the way we've always done it, and that's the way we're going to continue to do it!
- "No one is going to go for that!"
- "That's too risky, and there's no guarantee of success."
- "Why change? Things are fine just the way they are."
- "That's going to be too hard for us to do."

Did you notice that the phrases of the team members who are the "old dogs" mimic the phrases of a leader bent on resisting change? Another one slipped through the cracks and was promoted!

In addition to mimicking the leader who is resistant to change, you'll also hear the "old dog" using these doomsday predictions:

- If we do that, we're going to lose our customers."
- "If we listen to you, the whole company will be destroyed."
- "That's stupid. My friend, Sandra, worked at ABC Corporation and when they did that Sandra and a few others looked like fools."

HOW TO AVOID THIS MISTAKE:
Danger and Opportunity

In remarks delivered at the Convocation of the United Negro College Fund, Indianapolis, Indiana, April 12, 1959, then Senator John F. Kennedy incorrectly stated that, "When written in Chinese, the word "crisis" is composed of two characters—one represents danger and one represents opportunity." Actually, from all of my research, the Chinese word for change *appears* to be two characters: danger and opportunity. I'm not even sure if that's entirely true since I don't write or read Chinese! The closet I've come to China was a two-week speaking and training tour a while back in

Japan. I am sure about the truth of the statement that change does bring with it danger and opportunity. As a leader, your job is to see and be prepared for both.

Again, I'm going to pull from the four strategies I teach in my Women's Leadership Conferences.

- *Recognize and acknowledge the impact of change.* Change impacts people differently. Some team members will want to embrace the change; other team members will want to avoid the change. Your job is to recognize this and let your team know that whatever they're feeling is okay.
- *Tweak along the way.* Tweak is defined as "improve by making fine adjustments." You and your team will have to make adjustments as you settle into change. Because you are their leader, you must provide guidance and direction as to what adjustments—those tweaks, if you will—need to be made and when to make them. Change is not a straight path, and your team will need you to make some tweaks along the way.
- *Lower stress levels.* I once worked in the branch office of a major company as an Administrative Manager. Our home office was in Texas; I worked in Connecticut. All was going well until the home office decided to close my office and tasked me with the job of laying off thirteen employees...I made

thirteen! Talk about stress! I was stressed as were the employees I had to let go.

- o Here's what I learned: it is imperative to find practical ways to handle the stress of change. During that time I worked to help my team find new jobs. I gave them time off with pay. I made sure I provided a great reference for those who deserved it.

- o Change can be stressful. Help your team to lower their stress levels. Send the message that as a leader you care about them and what they may be going through.

- **Let people know what's going on.** As much as possible, you should let your team know what's happening as you all traverse this unknown territory called change. There are three stages of change: endings, transitions/neutral zone, and beginnings.

  - o First, all change begins with an ending—something ends and you have to let it go. *For example, your old job ended. You cannot go back there on Monday morning because you don't work there anymore.*

  - o Second, all change has a middle or the transition. During the transition you must take the time to complete the ending and begin a new pattern. Let's use the job example again. *You've started your new job but you don't feel 100% comfortable with how to lead your team meetings effectively. The first time you go without an agenda and discover that doesn't work. The next meeting you have an agenda and have assigned certain tasks to certain team members. It's a smashing success. Congratulations! You've just established a new pattern for your new job.*

o   Third, all change begins somewhere. This is the easiest to explain because it shows us that change is cyclical in nature. Back to the new job example: *You were hired by ABC Corporation.*

When you keep your team members abreast of the phases of changes, you are creating a bond based on trust. You're helping your team make better sense of and make better choices regarding the changes.

Recognize that change is the reality of a well-run team. Change gives you and your team the opportunity to grow, so embrace it. You can prepare your team for change if you will lead them in thinking about "life after change," rather than focusing on the way we used to do it. Help your team get out of their comfort zones. How? Insist they become strategic thinkers and get out of the ruts they may have created for themselves and the team.

LEAD LIKE A WOMAN:
Flex Your Mental Muscle

One of the things that frighten us about change is the nagging feeling of uncertainty that accompanies it. Uncertainty is synonymous with ambiguity. It's during those times that you, as a woman in leadership, should remember your natural abilities:

- You are naturally equipped to tolerate ambiguity.
- You possess the natural talent of mental flexibility.

I don't mention these qualities to imply that men aren't able to tolerate ambiguity or don't have mental flexibility. I believe women and men possess both. However, according to Dr. Helen Fisher these qualities are "some of the biological underpinnings of women's natural leadership talents." Fisher states further in the book *Enlightened Power*:

> *"Psychologists report that when women cogitate, [Author's note: Cogitate is a fancy word that means think] they gather details somewhat differently than men. Women integrate more details faster and arrange these bits of data into more complex patterns. As they make decisions, women tend to weigh more variables, consider more options, and see a wider array of possible solutions to a problem."*

If what psychologists report is true, it sounds to me like women leaders are pretty good at dealing with the uncertainty of change and helping their teams adjust, thrive, and survive.

I told you earlier about the job where I had to lay off the entire staff, including myself. Even though I did my best to take care of my employees, there were times when I was overwhelmed with the fact that I didn't know how things were going to work out. I wanted to control every step. I wanted to know that I was doing the right thing. What stands out the most about this major change in my life and my career was how I instinctively worked through what I felt needed to happen to make the change as palatable as possible. It was during this time I decided to complete my education and eventually open my own training and consulting business.

Lead like a woman and engage your team in whole-task thinking to encourage solutions. Help your team see the positive possibilities that could result from the change. Your team has to be able to adapt to and accept change. How you implement change will determine how easy adapting and accepting will be.

When change is needed, embrace it and verbalize your hopes and beliefs to your team. Use your mental flexibility to help your team deal with change and to become comfortable with the concept. Because you, as a woman, tend to weigh more variables, consider more options, and see a wider array of possible solutions to a problem, you have what it takes to help your team deal with the changes that will inevitably come. Flex on, my sister!

LEADERSHIP SELF-ASSESSMENT

*How do you measure up? Use this page to
objectively assess yourself and your team. Download your
Leadership Assessment Guide at: kbpbjz.bookhip.com*

Bibliography

Leadership Lesson One: Keep Them in the Dark

- [Elston, Kim]. (2014, January 6) *The Power of Words A Girl Changed a Blind Man Amazing.* [Video File]. Retrieved from https://www.youtube.com/watch?v=QYcXTlGLUgE

- Coughlin, L., Wingard, E., & Hollihan, Keith. (2005). The Natural Leadership Talents of Women. *Enlightened Power: How Women Are Transforming the Practice of Leadership* (pp. 133-140). San Francisco, CA: Josey-Bass.

- http://www.nationalpopularvote.com/written-explanation (National Popular Vote) Retrieved 6/11/2016.

- [wesawthat...]. (2012, October 23) *Hillary Clinton 2008 Democratic National Convention Speech.* [Video File]. Retrieved from https://www.youtube.com/watch?v=hRPCkyqJT1 4

- Tappero, Julie. Cliques in the Workplace. http://www.westsoundworkforce.com/cliques-in-the-workplace/ Retrieved June 11, 2016.

Leadership Lesson Two: Confusion Rules the Day

- Coughlin, L., Wingard, E., & Hollihan, Keith. (2005). The Natural Leadership Talents of Women. *Enlightened Power: How Women Are Transforming the Practice of Leadership* (pp. 133-140). San Francisco, CA: Josey-Bass.

- Secretary of State Hillary Clinton's Speech. January 22, 2009. Remarks to Department Employees at Welcome Event. Washington, DC. http://www.state.gov/secretary/20092013clinton/rm/ Retrieved May 4, 2014.

- Turner, K. The Science Behind Intuition: Why you should trust your gut. Published May 20, 2014. Psychology Today. Retrieved from https://www.psychologytoday.com/blog/radical-remission/201405/the-science-behind-intuition

Leadership Lesson Three: It's Not My Job

- Coughlin, L., Wingard, E., & Hollihan, Keith. (2005). The Natural Leadership Talents of Women. *Enlightened Power: How Women Are Transforming the Practice of Leadership* (pp. 133-140). San Francisco, CA: Josey-Bass.

- Dittmar, K., & Carr, G. (2016, March 25). Black Women Voters: By the Numbers. [Web log post]. Retrieved from http://www.huffingtonpost.com/kelly-dittmar/black-women-voters-by-the_b_9389330.html

- McDonald, S. (2011, January 11). Holistic Leadership: Understanding the Approach. [Web log post]. Retrieved from http://leadershiphq.com.au/wp-content/uploads/2011/02/holistic-leadership.pdf

- Parker, S. (2014, November 10). First Lady Michelle Obama Honors Women Veterans [Web log post]. Retrieved from https://www.whitehouse.gov/blog/2014/11/10/first-lady-michelle-obama-honors-women-veterans

- Pierce, C. P. (2015, December 28). Why Hillary Clinton's Stint as a Civil-Rights Secret Agent Matters Today. [Web log post]. Retrieved from http://www.esquire.com/news-politics/politics/news/a40772/hillary-clinton-undercover-civil-rights/

- Turner, C. Hands-on Leadership. Expert Trusted Advisor. (2011, August 29). [Web log post]. Retrieved from http://experttrustedadvisor.com/hands-on-leadership.20.207.resource.html.

Leadership Lesson Four: Everyone is Inadequate

- Coughlin, L., Wingard, E., & Hollihan, Keith. (2005). The Natural Leadership Talents of Women. *Enlightened Power: How Women Are Transforming the*

Practice of Leadership (pp. 133-140). San Francisco, CA: Josey-Bass.

Leadership Lesson Five: Forget About Accountability

- Coughlin, L., Wingard, E., & Hollihan, Keith. (2005). The Natural Leadership Talents of Women. *Enlightened Power: How Women Are Transforming the Practice of Leadership* (pp. 133-140). San Francisco, CA: Josey-Bass.

- Johnson, A. A Story of Personal Responsibility As A Leader. (2010, August 10). [Web log post]. Retrieved from https://coachaljohnson.wordpress.com/category/career-ownership/

- Kouzes, J.M., & Posner, B.Z. (2002). The Leadership Challenge. San Francisco, CA: Josey-Bass.

- National Susan B. Anthony Museum & House. [Web log post]. Retrieved May 24, 2015 from http://susanbanthonyhouse.org/her-story/biography.php#suff

- Sapadin, L. Do You Know Someone with Responsibility Deficit Disorder? (2013, April 3). [Web log post]. Retrieved from http://psychcentral.com/blog/archives/2013/04/03/do-you-know-someone-with-responsibility-deficit-disorder/

- Why Women Leaders Can and Should be Authentic. (2008). *RHR International Executive Insights Newsletter, 23*, 3.

Leadersip Lesson Six: It's All About Freedom

- Helgesen, S. The Female Advantage. (1995). New York, NY: Bantam Doubleday Dell.

- Inclusion [Def. 1]. (n.d.). *Merriam-Webster Online.* In Merriam-Webster. Retrieved January 2, 2013, from http://www.merriam-webster.com/dictionary/inclusion.

- Vulcan, N. How to Deal With an Employee Who is Trying to Sabotage You. Retrieved March 12, 2014 [Web log post] from http://woman.thenest.com/deal-employee-trying-sabotage-6122.html

Leadership Lesson Seven:
Make Sure They Die on the Vine

- Goleman, D. Working with Emotional Intelligence. (2006). New York, NY: Bantam Dell.

- Jacqui, T. The Six Types of Motivation (2008, August 27). [Web log post]. Retrieved from https://theofficenewb.wordpress.com/2008/08/27/the-six-types-of-motivation/

- Kelly, D. Why People Hate Training and How to Overcome It. (2012, March 6). [Web log post]. Retrieved from https://www.mindflash.com/blog/why-people-hate-training-and-how-to-overcome-it/

- People skills. (n.d.). *Business Dictionary Online.* In Business Skills Dictionary. Retrieved June 1, 2016, from http://www.businessdictionary.com/definition/people-skills.html

- Really Bad Jokes #205. (n.d.). [Web log post]. Retrieved August 30, 2012 from http://www.rinkworks.com/jokes/jokes21.shtml

Leadership Lesson Eight: You Can Trust Me...*Really*!

- Bennis, W. (2003). On Becoming a Leader. Philadelphia, PA: Perseus Books Group.

- Burns, J.M. (1978). Leadership. New York, NY: Harper & Row.
- Eagly, A. (2013). Retrieved from http://www.hbs.edu/faculty/conferences/2013-w50-research-symposium/Documents/eagly.pdf

- Meyers, S. 7 Signs of People With Integrity. (2015, April 6). [Web log post]. Retrieved from https://www.psychologytoday.com/blog/insight-is-2020/201504/7-signs-people-integrity

Leadership Lesson Nine: No Creativity Allowed

- Brainstorming [Def. 1]. (n.d.). *Merriam-Webster Online.* In Merriam-Webster. Retrieved June 19, 2016, from http://www.merriam-webster.com/dictionary/inclusion.

- Curtis, S. The Innovations that Took Amazon From Online Bookseller To Dominant Global Marketplace. (2013, October 15). [Web log post].

Retrieved from
http://www.businessinsider.com/the-innovations-that-took-amazon-from-online-bookseller-to-dominant-global-marketplace-2013-10

- Kjerulf, A. Kill the Suggestion Box—There's a Much Better Way. (2014, February 10). [Web log post]. Retrieved from http://positivesharing.com/2014/02/kill-suggestion-box-heres-much-better-way/

- Lofgren, K. 2016 Video Game Statistics & Trends Who's Playing What & Why. (2016, February 8). [Web log post]. Retrieved from http://www.bigfishgames.com/blog/2016-video-game-statistics-and-trends/

- Sena, P. Breaking Up with Brainstorming: How Gamestorming Helps Build an Innovation Culture. (2015, November 5). [Web log post]. Retrieved from http://marketeer.kapost.com/how-gamestorming-helps-build-an-innovation-culture/

- Sherwin, B. Why Women are More Effective Leaders Than Men. (2014, January 24). [Web log post]. Retrieved from http://www.businessinsider.com/study-women-are-better-leaders-2014-1

- Shontell, A. Meet Ben Silbermann, The Brilliant Young Co-founder of Pinterest. (2012, May 5). [Web log post]. Retrieved from http://www.businessinsider.com/pinterest-2012-3

- Wolf, G. Steve Jobs: The Next Insanely Great Thing. (1996, February 1). [Web log post]. Retrieved from http://www.wired.com/1996/02/jobs-2/

Leadership Lesson Ten: We've Never Done it Like That Before

- Blockbuster LLC. (n.d.). In *Wikipedia*. Retrieved October 14, 2012, from http://en.wikipedia.org/wiki/Blockbuster_LLC

- Coughlin, L., Wingard, E., & Hollihan, Keith. (2005). The Natural Leadership Talents of Women. *Enlightened Power: How Women Are Transforming the Practice of Leadership* (pp. 133-140). San Francisco, CA: Josey-Bass.

- Senator John F. Kennedy's Remarks. April 12, 1959. Remarks at the Convocation of the United Negro College Fund, Indianapolis, Indiana. Retrieved July 21, 2015. http://www.jfklibrary.org/Research/Research-Aids/JFK-Speeches/Indianapolis-IN_19590412.aspx

- http://www.vox.com/culture/2016/7/14/12190170/pokemon-go-ios-android-adult-age

ABOUT THE AUTHOR

D r. Angela Massey is a bold, energetic, confident woman who can help make a difference in your organization. As an experienced communicator having worked for clients such as IBM, Dell Corporation, Yale University, and Federal Express, Dr. Angela brings enthusiasm and energy to her presentations. Lovingly referred to as *The Gap Closer*, Dr. A's audiences are captivated by her presence, wit, and down-to-earth personality. In a word, Dr. A is real! Her skill at using everyday situations and humorous anecdotes to communicate her message makes her presentations unique, relevant, practical, and fun! The corporate training, development, and coaching sessions that Dr. Massey provides are guaranteed to energize, excite and motivate your organization to close their personal and professional gaps and open their personal and professional greatness!

Call Dr. Angela at (860) 478-4220 to schedule a consultation. Visit her website at: www.drangelamassey.com.

www.ingramcontent.com/pod-product-compliance
Lightning Source LLC
LaVergne TN
LVHW021502080426
835509LV00018B/2371